God's Storehouse Principle

Workbook

Sheila Holm

God's Storehouse Principle

Copyright © 2014 Sheila Holm

ISBN-10:1496022688

ISBN-13:978-1496022684

Unless otherwise indicated all scriptures are taken from the

New King James version of the Bible.

HISBest4us@aol.com

Printed in USA by HIS Best Publishing

Dedication, In Grateful Acknowledgment

To the memory of my Father (1918-2011) who did not lose faith in the midst of crisis and always taught us to do the right thing and my Mother who has taught by example, Irvin and Clarice, and to my California family, my cousins LaVonne and Gene McGee, and to our ancestors who emigrated to America for religious freedom and stood firm in faith.

To Bishop George Dallas McKinney for the depth of prophetic understanding required to merely lay his hands upon the back side of the draft manuscript, while it was merely an introductory letter God had me prepare before our 'meeting in three days,' for knowing the content and names (not included) before reading words, for being steadfast in helping me to keep on keepin' on, personally, encouraging me prior to and after each new adventure with God, while I remain grateful for your stand for all whom God sends to you!

To the memory (1918-2006) of Pastor Harald Bredesen, the friendship developed during meetings with and introductions arranged by him, especially for setting up my interview with Benny Hinn. For sharing front row studio seats because God orchestrated my attendance as a witness of the prophetic word from Benny Hinn that God would send a Muslim man with a salvation testimony and his name would be Nasir (Dr. Nasir Siddiki).

To Pastor Steve Dittmar, Jubilee Church, and to my host families during my visits, especially to Michael and Wendy Blomquist and to the powerful testimony of Christina Thee to confirm the faith level of children at four years old, and to her family for providing the Tommy Tenney books, plus to the many prayer partners and the multiple blessings received by participating at Jubilee after each assignment 'in a new way' as orchestrated by God.

To Pastor Greg & Patricia Young, Collynn and adoption into the Young family and in these details we must acknowledge the oldest Young, Michelle.

To Pastor Earl Harrigan for being an amazing, anointed singer, especially *Walk on the Water* and *All Rise,* plus being a key witness to these days.

To Big John Hall for confirming God introduced us at a Rodney Howard Browne meeting & positioned us in each others' 'hometown' for HIS purpose!

To John Willison for his mighty testimony, offer to provide a tour of the TBN studio in Irving, Texas, a tour which has not happened, yet, however, it led to an introduction with the TBN producer, opportunity to be interviewed on *Praise The Lord,* and for being the pilot who provided travel to a women's conference in Arkansas and to the Oklahoma church to encourage a pastor who was also from Nebraska. By the way, I'm still waiting for the promised tour of TBN.

To Ken Blanchard, for understanding exactly where my life was and what was required to get me out from under the rock to stand firm on the rock once again while living beyond the 'world plans' by diving 100% into Kingdom business!

To Rodney Howard Browne for returning many times to San Diego at the exact time to renew the anointing that restores and prepares me to say YES for the next assignment.

To TD Jakes and Pastor Sam Ankrah, Pastor Charles Benneh and staff, to Bishop Duncan Williams and to his worship team, and to singers Noel Robinson for depth of worship & Osene who took us into the glory with the first note.

To the Pastors & Bishops in London, and to Bishop John Francis for sharing the gift of his *Finally* CD, for the amazing contributions made during my journey.

To Pastor Mark Smallcomb for understanding the depth of *God's Storehouse Principle* message, yielding to God's structure, inviting me to share the details with business leaders and surrounding churches, including me within the Ed Silvoso meetings and for proclaiming the testimony of what God did when we came together on national TV (Australian version of CBS 60 Minutes).

To Pastor Rex Morgan for yielding to God so the Aboriginal Community could hear the message of *God's Storehouse Principle* and support the implementation during the service.

To Pastor Arnold in London for being so deeply touched by the message within *God's Storehouse Principle* that you were seeking the best of the best audio options to give me a copy so it would re-encourage me in the exact moment when I needed re-encouragement.

To Pastor Isileli for capturing **God's Storehouse Principle** before gathering the church together for fasting and prayer and remaining diligent until God confirmed it was time for us to meet together for God would change a nation if we stood firm together with our Lord.

To Prophet and Apostle John Kelly for prophetic words over my life and for referring me to Pastor Harold Dewberry. To Pastor Harold Dewberry for standing firm, delivering and releasing so many from what binds their heart and mind and returns them to a real relationship with Christ, for fasting and praying until God shared a clear message about me traveling down under and remaining in the country long enough for God to orchestrate the time and opportunity for me to meet with the Pastor in Fiji, a trip which unfolded weeks after you left your laptop with me and returned to America.

To the pastors, evangelists, teachers, and fellow prophets and apostles, and the leadership of the church, the speakers and saints participating in the various seminars and conferences around the world who have invited me, encouraged me, prayed with me and introduced me to host families who have become part of my breath of life gift from God.

To the many pastors, evangelists, teachers, fellow prophets and apostles, and the leadership of the church, the speakers and saints participating in the various seminars and conferences around the world who have invited me, encouraged me, prayed with me and introduced me to host families who have become part of my breath of life gift from God.

To Kirk & Joni Bovill for their music, to the prayer partners, intercessors and prayer warriors walking the wall: Calvin Jackson, Paul Davis, Carol Marfori, Lisa Hauri, to the memory of Jan Franklin (leaving us too soon, December 7, 2008), a powerful prayer warrior who walked the wall and joined me as a witness for all of the California meetings and she became a valued prayer assistant with the long prayer lines, to Gary & Cindy Graham and to the memory (1953-2011) of 'Rozi' Graham Blegen, because in our lives as we gather together **It's A Faith Walk!** with the Holy Spirit confirming our personal part within **God's Storehouse Principle.**

ACKNOWLEDGMENTS

AFRICA

Ghana, West Africa

Pastor Sam

> *"Truly, God has sent you to us with a strong word for our church."*

Pastor Charles

> *"It blesses my soul to hear of your faith & see the fruit of the ministry."*

Johannesburg, South Africa

Pastor Jhanni

> *"God is doing a good work through you and I pray with you & our church."*

Coronation Ceremony

AUSTRALIA

Newcastle, New South Wales, Australia

Pastor Mark

> *"...the staff and business leaders heard the message of Personal & Professional Life Management this week, so we are blessed you agreed to preach the word to our church this morning."*

Prayer Team Meeting

> *"We know now how we will we be able to continue this mighty work when you are not in our midst..."*

Four Square Gospel Church, Aboriginal Cultural Center

Pastor Rex

"God blessed us through your preaching on Easter Sunday. We will never forget that you were in our midst ... God brought new people to Jesus today & we thank God for what He has done because you answered His call."

ENGLAND

London, England

Pastor Vincent, Glory House, East London

"...the honor is ours this Easter Sunday."

Associate Pastor

> ***"The Glory of our God Almighty shines upon you and through you in your speaking and your actions…we give Him praise."***

Protocol Team

> ***"God has mightily blessed us, by sending you into our midst."***

Pastor Arnold,

> ***"You have blessed the people of this congregation, and in His wisdom and timing, may He bring you back into our midst again, very soon."***

Pastor, West London

> **"We rejoice with you in hearing and seeing the mighty things God is doing."**

Pastor, *South London*

> **"Our God is evidenced in your life and your speaking, while we continue to thank God for the work He is doing through you..."**

High Commissioner, Kingdom of Tonga, serving in the Embassy in London, England; Ambassador, Akosita

> **"God's timing is always right...for you to be with us, prior to the Economic Summit, to meet and pray with us..."**

Sunderland, England

Anglican, Former Church of Pastor Smith Wigglesworth

Pastor Day

> *"I thank God for sending you to our church this morning, for serving communion to me, and for renewing and restoring me for the call upon my life."*

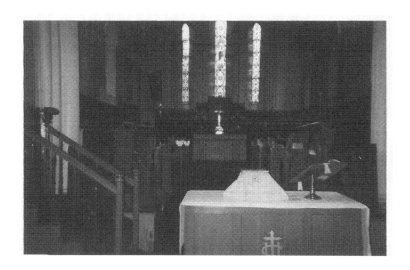

Kingdom of TONGA

Pastor Isileli Taukolo

> *"Our board and business leaders were fasting and praying and God confirmed He was sending someone to us. We are deeply touched by the message God sent to us, through you."*

Minister of Finance, Tasi

> *"Our meeting was an answer to my prayers, and I thank you for providing the seminar for our senior staff members, and meeting with them individually for prayer and coaching."*

Government Office

> *"Thank you for speaking today and for staying and praying with us."*

Interpreter, Sela

AMERICA

Man of God (Georgia), Requesting to be Discipled while attending the coronation of a King in Africa, Georgia

> *"...at my age, it is hard to believe I am learning so much in these few days about what I did not know...realizing what it is to know that I know how it is to live within God's word each day. Will you consider discipling me?"*

Pastor, Host of "Praise the Lord", TBN

> *"...The fruit of the ministry is evident in your testimony..."*

International Prophet

> *"You have remained steadfast to God's plan and God will continue to send you forth for His plan and purpose to be fulfilled, and for the thousands who have not knelt..."*

President, Christian Publishing Company

> *"Only God could orchestrate such a grand plan..."*

Prayer Director, International Prayer Center

> *"God is opening many doors for you..."*

Christian Publisher

"God has given you a powerful voice and a sweet spirit..."

Pastor, Southern California

"God is raising you up and sending you forth to many nations..."

International Apostle

"God is doing a mighty work through you, for His righteousness precedes you, showers over you and follows you as a mighty wake. May it continue for each of your days..."

Prophetic Prayer Partner, Minnesota

"Only God could walk you through these days...accomplish so much through you, in the midst of your daily situations, the many blessings shared during each of your travels will continue to shower blessings upon each of the many households around the world..."

God's Storehouse Principle

Testimonials

Business to Business, Nation to Nation

B. Crousure, President
Medical Corporation

"Hiring Ms. Holm to help me structure my first business was the brightest decision I have made. She taught me how to understand what success demands of me and she trained me how to operate at her level of commitment, while expressing an intense passion for my life and for the business, and to significantly contribute to the community. Without her coaching, I know my wife, my team and I would still be standing squarely in the lackluster mire she found us in, today, instead of our business being rated on the New York Stock Exchange (NYSE). Her coaching techniques were the turning point for our lives and for our company. We have catapulted into and experienced fantastic growth, both internally and externally. We anticipated receiving help with business systems, however, her extensive experience in balancing every area of our life first, and then inserting our business into our life has made a huge difference in our life and our bottom line. Her depth of knowledge in life and corporate structuring has been the key to our success. As a lifetime athlete, I should have made the connection to what coaching would mean to my business. It has been the "play book", the two-hour training sessions, the chalk talks before the game, and the champagne after the victories!"

P. Long, Post Office Employee
United States Post Office

"Coaching is nothing like consulting! We have met with a few consultants about each of our business tasks and how the work flow should progress. However, when I attended our conference and heard about a speaker who identified specific coaching techniques which could positively impact each aspect of my life...I laughed and said, 'I will not be in that session'. Then, when I walked down

the hallway, I realized something was going on, since the <u>only</u> place left in the room, was an opening to lean against the wall. I'm so glad I walked in...every aspect of my life has been impacted positively, since I heard Ms. Holm speak that evening. I thank you, and my family and my co-workers thank you!"

R. Oliver, Executive Vice President
Utility Company

"My staff had always attended the seminars, while I budgeted and selected the people to attend. However, I did not attend. I did not realize, until the first two hour session with Ms. Holm, I had always delegated the daily assignments at the office <u>and</u> at home, especially when I stated that I <u>let</u> my wife adopt two daughters. We had help at home, I had help at the office, and all of the daily needs were met. However, I did not have an "extra" ordinary life! I did not have a meaningful relationship with anyone, including myself, until I met Ms. Holm. Nothing about my life is the same, since the first moments we met and I heard her speak about the TIME secret. I have gained an ability to relate personally to the people in my daily life. Our daughters now fight to sit closest to me. The results have been amazing, and I will always be grateful."

C. Lynch, Corporate Engineering Manger
Aerospace Industry, Entrepreneur and Owner

"I would still be working on my business plan and living without a life plan, for the first business instead of owning and operating three businesses today and enjoying an "extra" ordinary life, if I had not signed up for the Entrepreneurial Course with Ms. Holm. It was immediately evident in the course I did not have a successful plan for my day, let alone a plan for my life, my family <u>or</u> my business. My business ideas were innovative, as I am a successful engineer and manager. However, I was not aware of the techniques required to establish a plan for my life or for my business start-up or the required steps to ensure the success of my business through the various development phases. The practical information and

the step-by-step format of the coaching and the course made it possible to 'fill in the blanks' to establish my daily life plan, to fulfill upon my plans and goals, and to proceed with a successful business plan and structure, while I was supported by the coach, and now, I can easily update my life and business plan each day! Many thanks, coach!"

T. Lehman, President
Furniture Manufacturing, Distribution and Sales

"The division we targeted for closure this month received our annual EXCELLENCE in Performance award for being our most improved division. Through your coaching process, causing each of us to create powerful life plans and then powerful plans for our work projects, teams automatically developed and began functioning effectively and <u>profitably</u>. The value of the staff believing in themselves far exceeds our initial intended results! The initial project resulted in a 50% increase in production and a 30% increase in related sales within the first 90 days."

R. Tretsven, Owner
Beauty Supply, with Salon Services

"Prior to hearing Sheila speak, I absolutely did not have a life! I progressed through each day, each week and month, fighting to keep ahead of the bills. Each time the business level plateaued, I went into a panic, a spin, and adjusted each section of the business, ie., I would stop ordering products, or reduce the number of technicians or sales staff, or obtain a new or expanded credit line. Everything about my business, and my life, were "out of control" and "out of balance." Then, when I tried the scheduling and budgeting techniques she described, I immediately noticed an increase of 35% in business, and 100% in life."

J. Schneider, Vice President
Interior Design Corporation

"We not only gained your level of passion and energy for our life, we gained the same level of energy and passion for our business and everyone who contributes to it. We are excited about the many techniques we learned, to search for everyone our business can contribute to within our community! We also profited significantly from the insights which surfaced, while we were creating our business, marketing and operational plans together. Thanks for believing in us during our periods of doubt, causing us to obtain the ability to create and proceed upon dynamic personal goals and then exceed all expectations by producing results beyond our previous three and five year plans within the first project plan. We have learned to 'not dig up with doubt, the seeds we planted in faith'. Thanks for everything!"

T. Fakafanua, Minister of Finance
Kingdom of Tonga

"Within the first 30 minutes of being introduced to Sheila, I scheduled a seminar and individual coaching sessions for our top 30 department heads and Treasury Department senior staff members. The timing was perfect, as we needed to restructure our policies, procedures and the entire operating plan, within the next 30 days. Ms. Holm provided a clear and practical outline for us to use, to structure our lives, our departments, and our government"

God's Storehouse Principle

Table of Contents

Page

Foreword

Sheila Holm has produced a concise statement on God's seeding and harvesting 'Kingdom Business' principle - a tithe of all - as God's master plan for stewardship, while she shares how she discovered *God's Storehouse Principle*.

Sheila's journey of faith begins with the recognition that 'we are totally and absolutely dependent upon God' and that God has predestined our lives for his purpose and provided a plan for us, which supports his work.

Armed with this knowledge and faith, Sheila becomes a yielded vessel to be God's ambassador to encourage Christians, especially pastors, throughout the US, Africa, Australia and Europe. Without sponsors or any visible means of support, she has traveled the world sustained by the faithfulness of God.

God's Storehouse Principle confirms God's wisdom and plan within the testimony, "*God supplies all that we are and all that we need and He requests that we bring tithes of all that He gives us...*" based on the truth "*...the Earth is the Lords and the Fullness thereof,*" Psalms 24:1-2, I Corinthians 10:26 and 28.

Since God is the owner of everything He has the right to establish the terms of stewardship imposed upon those entrusted with His property including all that we have been given: our life, time, treasure and talents. When *God's Storehouse Principle* is implemented, while we unite together, for each other, "*All of God's work done God's way will not lack God's supply.*"

God's Storehouse Principle is based upon God's plan that our blessings are to be shared so that the needs of others will be met, especially widows and orphans (all without husbands and fathers).

I strongly recommend *God's Storehouse Principle* for it is a timely and urgent call for every Christian to do all of our business God's way.

Bishop George Dallas McKinney

President, Pentecostal & Charismatic Churches North America (70,000+)

Board Member of Global Ministries: Billy Graham, Morris Cerullo, etc.

General Board Member, Church of God in Christ (COGIC)

Bishop and Pastor, St. Stephens Cathedral (COGIC)

Chapter 1   God's Storehouse Principle: Time

Set aside 'first fruits' of our daily 24/7 schedule; Plan to share with others

With God's guidance, 'Expanding Time; Contributing in a 24/7 world'

We have all of the time 'in the world' that we need, already!

It is the desire of God's heart for us to live aligned with ***God's Storehouse***

Principle so we will begin to hear and see what God has 'in store' for each of us:

1 Corinthians 2:9

"Eye has not seen, nor ear heard, nor have entered into the heart of man, the things which God has ('in store') prepared for those who love Him." (NIV) ... *"No eye has seen, no ear has heard, no mind has conceived what God has prepares ('in store'), for those who love him"*

Psalm 34:10 (NIV)

The lions may grow weak and hungry, but those who seek the Lord lack no good thing.

Time has represented the same structure through the generations, remaining exact through the centuries. God is absolutely "in the details" about time! The only 'break' in time represents the exact time Jesus Christ was on earth. In fact, all time is broken down into two segments, before and after birth:

All time BC: Before Christ, years prior to the birth of Christ

All time AD: Anno Domini, Year of our Lord (birth of Christ)

As humans, operating as humans, we are not able to begin to understand God's plans. Therefore, each day, we are to begin by spending time with God.

James 4:8 *Draw nigh to God, and he will draw nigh to you.*

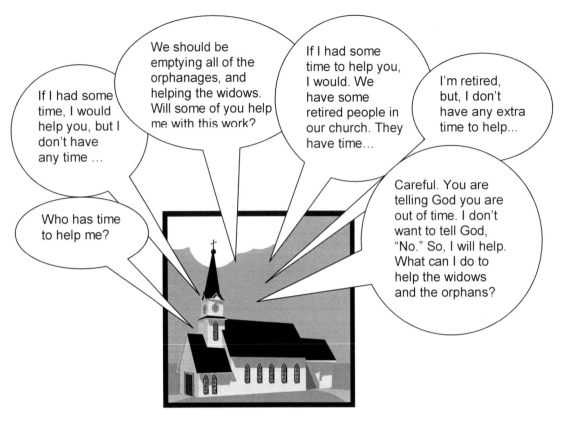

God's Secret about Time

Everything comes from God. Every moment in time is from God.

Every breath of our life comes from God. The last moment in our lifetime, here on earth, is when God grants our last breath. Sounds exhausting or difficult?

It is only going to be 'simple' when we 'let go, and let God' control our life, while we accept the counsel of the Holy Spirit, so we will all be ready to live *Aligned With God's Storehouse Principle,* as God is *"...no respecter of persons"* **Acts 10:34**

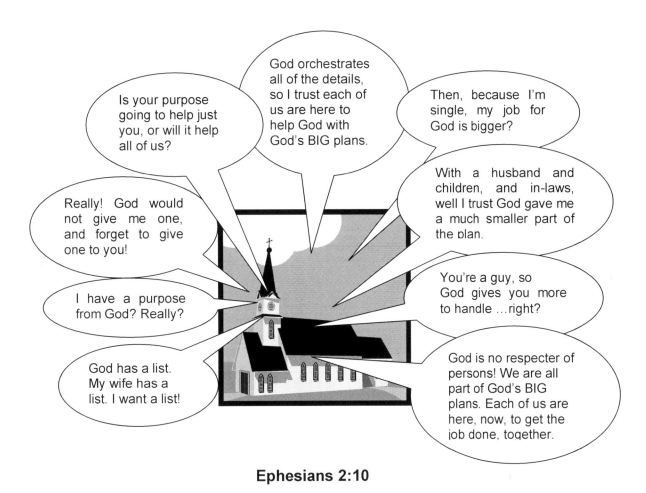

Ephesians 2:10

For we are God's workmanship, created in Christ Jesus, to do good works, which God prepared in advance for us to do."

I Corinthians 2:9

... "Eye has not seen, nor ear heard, nor have entered into the heart of man, the things which God has ('in store') prepared for those who love Him." (NIV) ... "For ear hath not heard, nor eye seen, nor can the mind begin to conceive the glory God has 'in store' for those who love Him."

God has seeded our lives and the lives of fellow believers with all that we need to fulfill upon God's plans for these days.

The good news:

God gives us a new day,

every day,

and an entire lifetime

to do our job!

First time the calendar was written 24/7, it required four pages of columns for the days of the week, and on the left side listing the time of day:

1) midnight to 6 AM,

2) 6 AM to noon,

3) noon to 6 PM, and

4) 6 PM to midnight.

When we look at the entire 24-hour calendar, we are able to use our perfect 20-20 vision by using hindsight to back into our daily schedule.

1. Insert our details in the four calendar pages;

2. Begin to see who we focus upon; how we spend our time each day;

3. Begin to see where time expands or it seems to leak out of our day.

Begin with our life first vs. our commitments to others. Then, identify hours at rest, preparing for work, driving to and from work, going out/staying in for lunch, and all of the time-consuming tasks.

1 Begin the day with a tithe of time to/with God, so the rest of the details are simply details; Prayers at the beginning of the day and prayers at the end of the day, listing the blessings from the storehouse and through us, as God's extension of the storehouse, help to expand your day and time of rest, and live the abundant life God's intends for us to live, in peace, joy and righteousness!

Each hour gives us a new opportunity to find six minutes, a tithe of the hour, to spend with God during that hour or at some point in our day, so we will know the surprises God has "in store" for us. Each 15 minute segment that is not scheduled for 'work' or 'rest' or 'pre-planned' events can be 'red lined' to hold it (aka 'storing time') open for your plans, either for time with God, family or as a 'gift' to/for others. You will begin to see, when you hold this time as 'important' and 'unavailable' to the world until <u>you decide</u> how it will be spent. People who use your time for phone calls or lengthy conversations about their lack of time (or focus) will begin to realize you have established specific boundaries. You will notice you have 'expanded your time.' When we honor our new schedule, others will want to hear God's secret about time! It's in our "human" nature!

Lie: The schedule that has been unfair to us is actually the 'world-based' eight, ten or 12-hour calendar. We try to squeeze everything into one-third to half of each day of our life.

Lie: Weekend days are half days or non-existent, especially Sundays. To God, that calendar is unacceptable. In fact, that calendar is a lie!

Truth: <u>When you treat each **'red lined' 15-minute time slot** on your 24-hour calendar the same way, it puts you back in the driver's seat of your life, helps you make choices about how you spend your time and how you contribute time to other people.</u>

Each 15 minute time slot can represent writing a note card to mail to someone, to encourage them, to email or call someone, to encourage them -- or limit the time to three, five minute calls, or as many as five, three minute calls (TEXT people who are 'talkers' so they are encouraged without requiring time to chat about the message), to bless the people you hold most dear.

Oh yes, need I remind you to make an appointment with yourself. Be on time and treat it as important as the time you have scheduled for anyone else or anything else during your day.

Once you start the contribution cycle of blessings, it will gain momentum and the blessings will begin to flow back into your life.

A hint: God has shown me how to handle the 'problem people,' the people who are very negative or they want to take up all of your time and only talk about facts which bring you down. As they approach you, you can merely say, *"Bless you"* as you keep on keepin' on; Holy Spirit will take care of the rest!

This is how *God's Storehouse Principle* (contribution cycle) works.

Personal Responsibility

Matthew 6:33 (NIV)

… seek first his kingdom and his righteousness, and all these things will be given to you as well.

Using your birth date as a day of 'remembrance,' make a list of the number of years in the left column.

Write a note next to each year regarding moments you remember on your Birthday that year.

Then, add a note about memories created in that year and people who created memories with you during the year. You may need to view photos or ask relatives about the earliest years.

1.

Birthday

Memories Created

People Who Created Memories

2.

Birthday

Memories Created

People Who Created Memories

3.

Birthday

Memories Created

People Who Created Memories

4.

Birthday

Memories Created

People Who Created Memories

5.

Birthday

Memories Created

People Who Created Memories

6.

Birthday

Memories Created

People Who Created Memories

7.

Birthday

Memories Created

People Who Created Memories

8.

Birthday

Memories Created

People Who Created Memories

9.

Birthday

Memories Created

People Who Created Memories

10.

Birthday

Memories Created

People Who Created Memories

------------Decade of life

Who discipled you during this decade?

Who did you disciple within this decade?

11.

Birthday

Memories Created

People Who Created Memories

12.

Birthday

Memories Created

People Who Created Memories

13.

Birthday

Memories Created

People Who Created Memories

14.

Birthday

Memories Created

People Who Created Memories

15.

Birthday

Memories Created

People Who Created Memories

16.

Birthday

Memories Created

People Who Created Memories

17.

Birthday

Memories Created

People Who Created Memories

18.

Birthday

Memories Created

People Who Created Memories

19.

Birthday

Memories Created

People Who Created Memories

20.

Birthday

Memories Created

People Who Created Memories

------------Decade of life

Who discipled you during this decade?

Who did you disciple within this decade?

21.

Birthday

Memories Created

People Who Created Memories

22.

Birthday

Memories Created

People Who Created Memories

23.

Birthday

Memories Created

People Who Created Memories

24.

Birthday

Memories Created

People Who Created Memories

25.

Birthday

Memories Created

People Who Created Memories

26.

Birthday

Memories Created

People Who Created Memories

27.

Birthday

Memories Created

People Who Created Memories

28.

Birthday

Memories Created

People Who Created Memories

29.

Birthday

Memories Created

People Who Created Memories

30.

Birthday

Memories Created

People Who Created Memories

------------Decade of life

Who discipled you during this decade?

Who did you disciple within this decade?

31.

Birthday

Memories Created

People Who Created Memories

32.

Birthday

Memories Created

People Who Created Memories

33.

Birthday

Memories Created

People Who Created Memories

34.

Birthday

Memories Created

People Who Created Memories

35.

Birthday

Memories Created

People Who Created Memories

36.

Birthday

Memories Created

People Who Created Memories

37.

Birthday

Memories Created

People Who Created Memories

38.

Birthday

Memories Created

People Who Created Memories

39.

Birthday

Memories Created

People Who Created Memories

40.

Birthday

Memories Created

People Who Created Memories

------------Decade of life

Who discipled you during this decade?

Who did you disciple within this decade?

41.

Birthday

Memories Created

People Who Created Memories

42.

Birthday

Memories Created

People Who Created Memories

43.

Birthday

Memories Created

People Who Created Memories

44.

Birthday

Memories Created

People Who Created Memories

45.

Birthday

Memories Created

People Who Created Memories

46.

Birthday

Memories Created

People Who Created Memories

47.

Birthday

Memories Created

People Who Created Memories

48.

Birthday

Memories Created

People Who Created Memories

49.

Birthday

Memories Created

People Who Created Memories

50.

Birthday

Memories Created

People Who Created Memories

------------Decade of life

Who discipled you during this decade?

Who did you disciple within this decade?

51.

Birthday

Memories Created

People Who Created Memories

52.

Birthday

Memories Created

People Who Created Memories

53.

Birthday

Memories Created

People Who Created Memories

54.

Birthday

Memories Created

People Who Created Memories

55.

Birthday

Memories Created

People Who Created Memories

56.

Birthday

Memories Created

People Who Created Memories

57.

Birthday

Memories Created

People Who Created Memories

58.

Birthday

Memories Created

People Who Created Memories

59.

Birthday

Memories Created

People Who Created Memories

60.

Birthday

Memories Created

People Who Created Memories

------------Decade of life

Who discipled you during this decade?

Who did you disciple within this decade?

61.

Birthday

Memories Created

People Who Created Memories

62.

Birthday

Memories Created

People Who Created Memories

63.

Birthday

Memories Created

People Who Created Memories

64.

Birthday

Memories Created

People Who Created Memories

65.

Birthday

Memories Created

People Who Created Memories

66.

Birthday

Memories Created

People Who Created Memories

67.

Birthday

Memories Created

People Who Created Memories

68.

Birthday

Memories Created

People Who Created Memories

69.

Birthday

Memories Created

People Who Created Memories

70.

Birthday

Memories Created

People Who Created Memories

------------Decade of life

Who discipled you during this decade?

Who did you disciple within this decade?

71.

Birthday

Memories Created

People Who Created Memories

72.

Birthday

Memories Created

People Who Created Memories

73.

Birthday

Memories Created

People Who Created Memories

74.

Birthday

Memories Created

People Who Created Memories

75.

Birthday

Memories Created

People Who Created Memories

76.

Birthday

Memories Created

People Who Created Memories

77.

Birthday

Memories Created

People Who Created Memories

78.

Birthday

Memories Created

People Who Created Memories

79.

Birthday

Memories Created

People Who Created Memories

80.

Birthday

Memories Created

People Who Created Memories

------------Decade of life

Who discipled you during this decade?

Who did you disciple within this decade?

81.

Birthday

Memories Created

People Who Created Memories

82.

Birthday

Memories Created

People Who Created Memories

83.

Birthday

Memories Created

People Who Created Memories

84.

Birthday

Memories Created

People Who Created Memories

85.

Birthday

Memories Created

People Who Created Memories

86.

Birthday

Memories Created

People Who Created Memories

87.

Birthday

Memories Created

People Who Created Memories

88.

Birthday

Memories Created

People Who Created Memories

89.

Birthday

Memories Created

People Who Created Memories

90.

Birthday

Memories Created

People Who Created Memories

------------Decade of life

Who discipled you during this decade?

Who did you disciple within this decade?

91.

Birthday

Memories Created

People Who Created Memories

92.

Birthday

Memories Created

People Who Created Memories

93.

Birthday

Memories Created

People Who Created Memories

.94.

Birthday

Memories Created

People Who Created Memories

95.

Birthday

Memories Created

People Who Created Memories

96.

Birthday

Memories Created

People Who Created Memories

97.

Birthday

Memories Created

People Who Created Memories

98.

Birthday

Memories Created

People Who Created Memories

99.

Birthday

Memories Created

People Who Created Memories

100.

Birthday

Memories Created

People Who Created Memories

------------Decade of life

Who discipled you during this decade?

Who did you disciple within this decade?

Amazing, isn't it, to realize how even the 'special days' in our lives become a blur. We can change this status. We can turn this situation around. **God's** plan: **Storehouse Principle** regarding time assists us with our 'memory bank' of time!

Each day, when we spend time with God and especially time praising God since God inhabits the praises of his people, **Psalms 22:3**, and we become available to hear from God through the counsel of the Holy Spirit, blessings flow. When we spend more time with God, we receive 'added value' in our time/life.

God gives us a specific structure each week: seven days. Each day is made up of two, twelve-hour segments. Each hour is sixty minutes. Each minute including sixty seconds. If we do not pay attention to what we do with the seconds, the minutes and hours will pass by, then, the days, weeks and months slip by. Then, before we know it, years slip by. Then, we lose memories about what happened within which year. Life becomes a blur, and we lose our focus, peace and joy. Clearly, we can rejoice about God's gift to us: the exact amount of time to live a great life, and then, we will begin to realize it is only God who can add years to our life! A couple of examples: **II Kings 20:6 and Isaiah 38:5.**

God's Secret: 'How to expand time.' Revealed!

God's secret about time is 'out of the bag' since it is being revealed to you, so your time will be spent wisely from this moment forward:

 # 1 step: Tithe your time issues to God. Begin by 'setting aside' the 'first fruits' of each 24-hour day, beginning with one of the 'red lined' 15 minutes, so you will 'over time' have 'more than enough time' to be with God, and to be counseled by the Holy Spirit. Then, you will find the 'extra' moments' to begin to live an 'expanded' aka 'extra' ordinary day/life, which is the desire of God's heart: Live an abundant life, and prosper!

 # 2 step: Contribute time by tithing time, giving it away per God's directions, to other people and to meet their needs, especially the widows & the orphans, since you receive a new 24 hour day, daily. This process confirms to us how God's blessings flow through us, touch the lives of others and bless us, once again. Contribution flow of time, in and out of our life, is the first step in the contribution flow of the Storehouse!

This is a new perspective that is only possible when life is being lived right side up and aligned with God's will and plan for our life. Did you notice that when God is the first priority, at the top of the "right side up" option, our time expands for each of the other areas of our daily life? In fact, time multiplies for the other people and priorities in our life! God's plans are good, and big, for each of us!

Examples: Preaching. God's perfect religion: care for widows & orphans.

WIDOWS (all without husbands): After service, two lists were prepared: 1. All services the people in the church can provide, i.e., mechanics, repair or handy work, dentists, doctors, attorneys, tutors, etc., 2. All services the people in the church need. The two lists, contribution and need, matched exactly! So, people started to find time in their schedules, to plan and contribute their services.

ORPHANS (all without fathers): A church heard this message and received letters from members within one month, 30 days: At least 30 children in the foster care system were with Christian families while the adoption process unfolds; families did not know the location of the orphanage in their community prior to the service. Also, men made a volunteer list for mentoring the youth in the congregation and the community. They were inspired by picking up the torch and taking on the opportunity to influence the next generation!

This is just one example, by sharing **God's Storehouse Principle** in one church, and then, receiving a report about what one church can do in one month!

God is very good at seeding the church to abundantly meet the need! In my **It's A Faith Walk!** book, I share a special seeding and harvesting of time example that met all of the needs of a church in Australia. Instead of $10,000 to meet the needs, they needed time from experienced welders. God provided the number of welders and time required to complete the job within the next week plus, God provided more than enough in the tithes and offerings!

Our Prayer

"Lord, you hear our voices, and you know our hearts. As humble and able servants, we are willing to tithe time to you each day, and to other people, to their needs, as you direct, to accept the promise Christ provided, to listen to and follow the counsel of the Holy Spirit. Father, thank you for aligning our will with yours, for the gift of a new day, every day, for more time to be with you, to plan our day, our life, our future, and to bless others. Thank you for the gift of hearing our voice clearly, as we walk in faith while we are still here on earth. In the name of our Lord & Savior Jesus Christ we pray, Amen

Storehouse Principle   Expanding Time   Action Plan

With 'hind sight' providing 20/20 Vision; Backing into the 24-hour daily schedule

1 Tithe of daily time, identifying our personal time with God, then:

Hours resting, preparing to begin and end each day

'Personal life,' relationship, family and daily time:

Personal LIFE, schedule for the day:

Intimate Relationship

Family

Reading (books, letters, and papers, etc.)

Communicating (by phone, email or letters, etc.)

Eating (time spent preparing & eating meals; driving to/from)

'Planning' LIFE:

Daily

Weekly or monthly events/trips, vacations

Contributing to other people and organizations in the community

'In Action' about LIFE:

Business/profession: work, at office/home, appointments, etc.

LIFE Plans, progressing on the plan

SAME for each of our weekend Hours

Separate distinctions for 'time' alone make a huge difference in how we view time! BALANCE of Weekly Time: LIVING A 24/7 LIFE: 24 hours X 7 = <u>168</u> hours

IS DAILY TIME BALANCED?

'Open time slots' are identified to <u>add</u> to the daily life plan as issues & events are known, they can be added!

'Extra' moments in time are identified, to support the change from an ordinary to an "extra" ordinary life.

New Calendar for a 24/7 life: 24 hour calendars for planning 'extra' ordinary days, noting every 15 minute segments of the hour, to match professional calendars, are used until the shift is made from using current eight to 12 hour calendars for the work week and partial or half days, or no time allotted, for weekends, to a weekly 24 hour calendar. A sample of the 24 hour calendar used after the shift is complete is provided:

Tithe of all!

Tithing while 'at rest!' YES!

You are in for a treat, if you have not requested God to put you into rest at the end of your day and wake you when he needs you, yet! Begin today!

1   Prepare the calendar by inserting your life, first & tithing!

  Time tithing your time

  Option to tithe six min. per hour

  While at the office, one min. per hour

   Remaining five from each hour prior to break

   Within your break time!

  God is amazing "in the min" when you "set aside" time!

2   Plan the remainder of your calendar & tithing

  Time for Planning your day/week/month/year

  Time for Planning events to share with those you hold dear

  Time to contribute to family, business, church, community

3   Prepare for a special day of work & tithing

  Time to accomplish the work/tasks

  Time to plan for the new work/tasks

  Time to work out details with co-workers

  Time to contribute to co-workers

  Training to improve upon the work/tasks

4   Time to REST & tithing of the resting hours

  Time prior to and immediately after rest for tithe?

 # 1. Invite God into your daily schedule

 # 2. Invite you back in,

and then, the people you hold dear,

 # 3. Invite the other people (more details in the People, Network chapter),

and then, the work and activities that truly help you fulfill upon

your purpose and plan for your life!

Bottom line:

God provides enough time

when He receives our 'first fruits' of our time!

It is time to practice for another month to be sure you have expanded your time, shifted your focus so your life is being lived right side up vs. upside down.

Right side up:

God

Relationship, Family, Friends

World News, Issues, Career, Worries

Upside down:

World News, Issues, Career, Worries

Relationship, Family, Friends

God

Week 1

MO___	MON	TUE	WED	THU	FRI	SAT	SUN
DATE							
12 AM							
12:15							
12:30							
12:45							
1							
1:15							
1:30							
1:45							
2							
2:15							
2:30							
2:45							
3							
3:15							
3:30							
3:45							
4							
4:15							
4:30							
4:45							
5							
5:15							
5:30							
5:45							
Total Hours:							
1) Personal + Tithing							
2) Planning + Tithing							
3) Working + Tithing							
4) At Rest + Tithing							

MO___ DATE	MON	TUE	WED	THU	FRI	SAT	SUN
6 AM							
6:15							
6:30							
6:45							
7							
7:15							
7:30							
7:45							
8							
8:15							
8:30							
8:45							
9							
9:15							
9:30							
9:45							
10							
10:15							
10:30							
10:45							
11							
11:15							
11:30							
11:45							
Total Hours:							
1) Planning + Tithing							
2) In Action + Tithing							
3) Personal + Tithing							
4) At Rest + Tithing							

God's Storehouse Principle

MO___ DATE	MON	TUE	WED	THU	FRI	SAT	SUN
12 Noon							
12:15							
12:30							
12:45							
1							
1:15							
1:30							
1:45							
2							
2:15							
2:30							
2:45							
3							
3:15							
3:30							
3:45							
4							
4:15							
4:30							
4:45							
5							
5:15							
5:30							
5:45							
Total Hours:							
1) Personal + Tithing							
2) Planning + Tithing							
3) Working + Tithing							
4) At Rest + Tithing							

© Sheila Holm

MO___ DATE	MON	TUE	WED	THU	FRI	SAT	SUN
6 PM							
6:15							
6:30							
6:45							
7							
7:15							
7:30							
7:45							
8							
8:15							
8:30							
8:45							
9							
9:15							
9:30							
9:45							
10							
10:15							
10:30							
10:45							
11							
11:15							
11:30							
11:45							
Total Hours:							
1) Personal + Tithing							
2) Planning + Tithing							
3) Working + Tithing							
4) At Rest + Tithing							

© *Sheila Holm*

Each month has an average of 4.33 weeks, so, after you practice with 24/7 days for a week, the option to insert your life each hour will start to become clear, so it becomes easier to identify; option to insert the key focus for each hour into the hour version:

MO___ DATE	MON	TUE	WED	THU	FRI	SAT	SUN
12 M							
1							
2							
3							
4							
5							
6							
7							
8							
9							
10							
11							
Noon							
1							
2							
3							
4							
5							
6							
7							
8							
9							
10							
11							
Total Hours:							
1) Personal + Tithing							
2) Planning + Tithing							
3) Working + Tithing							
4) At Rest + Tithing							

© Sheila Holm

WEEK 2

MO___	MON	TUE	WED	THU	FRI	SAT	SUN
DATE							
12 AM							
12:15							
12:30							
12:45							
1							
1:15							
1:30							
1:45							
2							
2:15							
2:30							
2:45							
3							
3:15							
3:30							
3:45							
4							
4:15							
4:30							
4:45							
5							
5:15							
5:30							
5:45							
Total Hours:							
1) Personal + Tithing							
2) Planning + Tithing							
3) Working + Tithing							
4) At Rest + Tithing							

MO___ DATE	MON	TUE	WED	THU	FRI	SAT	SUN
6 AM							
6:15							
6:30							
6:45							
7							
7:15							
7:30							
7:45							
8							
8:15							
8:30							
8:45							
9							
9:15							
9:30							
9:45							
10							
10:15							
10:30							
10:45							
11							
11:15							
11:30							
11:45							
Total Hours:							
1) Planning + Tithing							
2) In Action + Tithing							
3) Personal + Tithing							
4) At Rest + Tithing							

© Sheila Holm

MO___ DATE	MON	TUE	WED	THU	FRI	SAT	SUN
12 Noon							
12:15							
12:30							
12:45							
1							
1:15							
1:30							
1:45							
2							
2:15							
2:30							
2:45							
3							
3:15							
3:30							
3:45							
4							
4:15							
4:30							
4:45							
5							
5:15							
5:30							
5:45							
Total Hours:							
1) Personal + Tithing							
2) Planning + Tithing							
3) Working + Tithing							
4) At Rest + Tithing							

MO___ DATE	MON	TUE	WED	THU	FRI	SAT	SUN
6 PM							
6:15							
6:30							
6:45							
7							
7:15							
7:30							
7:45							
8							
8:15							
8:30							
8:45							
9							
9:15							
9:30							
9:45							
10							
10:15							
10:30							
10:45							
11							
11:15							
11:30							
11:45							
Total Hours:							
1) Personal + Tithing							
2) Planning + Tithing							
3) Working + Tithing							
4) At Rest + Tithing							

© Sheila Holm

Each month has an average of 4.33 weeks, so, after you practice with 24/7 days for a week, the option to insert your life each hour will start to become clear, so it becomes easier to identify; option to insert the key focus for each hour into the hour version:

MO___ DATE	MON	TUE	WED	THU	FRI	SAT	SUN
12 M							
1							
2							
3							
4							
5							
6							
7							
8							
9							
10							
11							
Noon							
1							
2							
3							
4							
5							
6							
7							
8							
9							
10							
11							
Total Hours:							
1) Personal + Tithing							
2) Planning + Tithing							
3) Working + Tithing							
4) At Rest + Tithing							

Week 3

MO___	MON	TUE	WED	THU	FRI	SAT	SUN
DATE							
12 AM							
12:15							
12:30							
12:45							
1							
1:15							
1:30							
1:45							
2							
2:15							
2:30							
2:45							
3							
3:15							
3:30							
3:45							
4							
4:15							
4:30							
4:45							
5							
5:15							
5:30							
5:45							
Total Hours:							
1) Personal + Tithing							
2) Planning + Tithing							
3) Working + Tithing							
4) At Rest + Tithing							

© *Sheila Holm*

MO___ DATE	MON	TUE	WED	THU	FRI	SAT	SUN
6 AM							
6:15							
6:30							
6:45							
7							
7:15							
7:30							
7:45							
8							
8:15							
8:30							
8:45							
9							
9:15							
9:30							
9:45							
10							
10:15							
10:30							
10:45							
11							
11:15							
11:30							
11:45							
Total Hours:							
1) Planning + Tithing							
2) In Action + Tithing							
3) Personal + Tithing							
4) At Rest + Tithing							

© Sheila Holm

MO___ DATE	MON	TUE	WED	THU	FRI	SAT	SUN
12 Noon							
12:15							
12:30							
12:45							
1							
1:15							
1:30							
1:45							
2							
2:15							
2:30							
2:45							
3							
3:15							
3:30							
3:45							
4							
4:15							
4:30							
4:45							
5							
5:15							
5:30							
5:45							
Total Hours:							
1) Personal + Tithing							
2) Planning + Tithing							
3) Working + Tithing							
4) At Rest + Tithing							

© Sheila Holm

MO___ DATE	MON	TUE	WED	THU	FRI	SAT	SUN
6 PM							
6:15							
6:30							
6:45							
7							
7:15							
7:30							
7:45							
8							
8:15							
8:30							
8:45							
9							
9:15							
9:30							
9:45							
10							
10:15							
10:30							
10:45							
11							
11:15							
11:30							
11:45							
Total Hours:							
1) Personal + Tithing							
2) Planning + Tithing							
3) Working + Tithing							
4) At Rest + Tithing							

© *Sheila Holm*

Each month has an average of 4.33 weeks, so, after you practice with 24/7 days for a week, the option to insert your life each hour will start to become clear, so it becomes easier to identify; option to insert the key focus for each hour into the hour version:

MO___ DATE	MON	TUE	WED	THU	FRI	SAT	SUN
12 M							
1							
2							
3							
4							
5							
6							
7							
8							
9							
10							
11							
Noon							
1							
2							
3							
4							
5							
6							
7							
8							
9							
10							
11							
Total Hours:							
1) Personal + Tithing							
2) Planning + Tithing							
3) Working + Tithing							
4) At Rest + Tithing							

© Sheila Holm

Week 4

MO___	MON	TUE	WED	THU	FRI	SAT	SUN
DATE							
12 AM							
12:15							
12:30							
12:45							
1							
1:15							
1:30							
1:45							
2							
2:15							
2:30							
2:45							
3							
3:15							
3:30							
3:45							
4							
4:15							
4:30							
4:45							
5							
5:15							
5:30							
5:45							
Total Hours:							
1) Personal + Tithing							
2) Planning + Tithing							
3) Working + Tithing							
4) At Rest + Tithing							

© Sheila Holm

MO___ DATE	MON	TUE	WED	THU	FRI	SAT	SUN
6 AM							
6:15							
6:30							
6:45							
7							
7:15							
7:30							
7:45							
8							
8:15							
8:30							
8:45							
9							
9:15							
9:30							
9:45							
10							
10:15							
10:30							
10:45							
11							
11:15							
11:30							
11:45							
Total Hours:							
1) Planning + Tithing							
2) In Action + Tithing							
3) Personal + Tithing							
4) At Rest + Tithing							

© *Sheila Holm*

MO___ DATE	MON	TUE	WED	THU	FRI	SAT	SUN
12 Noon							
12:15							
12:30							
12:45							
1							
1:15							
1:30							
1:45							
2							
2:15							
2:30							
2:45							
3							
3:15							
3:30							
3:45							
4							
4:15							
4:30							
4:45							
5							
5:15							
5:30							
5:45							
Total Hours:							
1) Personal + Tithing							
2) Planning + Tithing							
3) Working + Tithing							
4) At Rest + Tithing							

© Sheila Holm

MO___ DATE	MON	TUE	WED	THU	FRI	SAT	SUN
6 PM							
6:15							
6:30							
6:45							
7							
7:15							
7:30							
7:45							
8							
8:15							
8:30							
8:45							
9							
9:15							
9:30							
9:45							
10							
10:15							
10:30							
10:45							
11							
11:15							
11:30							
11:45							
Total Hours:							
1) Personal + Tithing							
2) Planning + Tithing							
3) Working + Tithing							
4) At Rest + Tithing							

© *Sheila Holm*

God's Storehouse Principle

Each month has an average of 4.33 weeks, so, after you practice with 24/7 days for a week, the option to insert your life each hour will start to become clear, so it becomes easier to identify; option to insert the key focus for each hour into the hour version:

MO___ DATE	MON	TUE	WED	THU	FRI	SAT	SUN
12 M							
1							
2							
3							
4							
5							
6							
7							
8							
9							
10							
11							
Noon							
1							
2							
3							
4							
5							
6							
7							
8							
9							
10							
11							
Total Hours:							
1) Personal + Tithing							
2) Planning + Tithing							
3) Working + Tithing							
4) At Rest + Tithing							

© *Sheila Holm*

God's Storehouse Principle

Week 5

MO___	MON	TUE	WED	THU	FRI	SAT	SUN
DATE							
12 AM							
12:15							
12:30							
12:45							
1							
1:15							
1:30							
1:45							
2							
2:15							
2:30							
2:45							
3							
3:15							
3:30							
3:45							
4							
4:15							
4:30							
4:45							
5							
5:15							
5:30							
5:45							
Total Hours:							
1) Personal + Tithing							
2) Planning + Tithing							
3) Working + Tithing							
4) At Rest + Tithing							

© Sheila Holm

MO___ DATE	MON	TUE	WED	THU	FRI	SAT	SUN
6 AM							
6:15							
6:30							
6:45							
7							
7:15							
7:30							
7:45							
8							
8:15							
8:30							
8:45							
9							
9:15							
9:30							
9:45							
10							
10:15							
10:30							
10:45							
11							
11:15							
11:30							
11:45							
Total Hours:							
1) Planning + Tithing							
2) In Action + Tithing							
3) Personal + Tithing							
4) At Rest + Tithing							

MO___ DATE	MON	TUE	WED	THU	FRI	SAT	SUN
12 Noon							
12:15							
12:30							
12:45							
1							
1:15							
1:30							
1:45							
2							
2:15							
2:30							
2:45							
3							
3:15							
3:30							
3:45							
4							
4:15							
4:30							
4:45							
5							
5:15							
5:30							
5:45							
Total Hours:							
1) Personal + Tithing							
2) Planning + Tithing							
3) Working + Tithing							
4) At Rest + Tithing							

MO___ DATE	MON	TUE	WED	THU	FRI	SAT	SUN
6 PM							
6:15							
6:30							
6:45							
7							
7:15							
7:30							
7:45							
8							
8:15							
8:30							
8:45							
9							
9:15							
9:30							
9:45							
10							
10:15							
10:30							
10:45							
11							
11:15							
11:30							
11:45							
Total Hours:							
1) Personal + Tithing							
2) Planning + Tithing							
3) Working + Tithing							
4) At Rest + Tithing							

Each month has an average of 4.33 weeks, so, after you practice with 24/7 days for a week, the option to insert your life each hour will start to become clear, so it becomes easier to identify; option to insert the key focus for each hour into the hour version:

MO___ DATE	MON	TUE	WED	THU	FRI	SAT	SUN
12 M							
1							
2							
3							
4							
5							
6							
7							
8							
9							
10							
11							
Noon							
1							
2							
3							
4							
5							
6							
7							
8							
9							
10							
11							
Total Hours:							
1) Personal + Tithing							
2) Planning + Tithing							
3) Working + Tithing							
4) At Rest + Tithing							

© Sheila Holm

Second Month of practice:
Week 1

MO___	MON	TUE	WED	THU	FRI	SAT	SUN
DATE							
12 AM							
12:15							
12:30							
12:45							
1							
1:15							
1:30							
1:45							
2							
2:15							
2:30							
2:45							
3							
3:15							
3:30							
3:45							
4							
4:15							
4:30							
4:45							
5							
5:15							
5:30							
5:45							
Total Hours:							
1) Personal + Tithing							
2) Planning + Tithing							
3) Working + Tithing							
4) At Rest + Tithing							

© Sheila Holm

MO___ DATE	MON	TUE	WED	THU	FRI	SAT	SUN
6 AM							
6:15							
6:30							
6:45							
7							
7:15							
7:30							
7:45							
8							
8:15							
8:30							
8:45							
9							
9:15							
9:30							
9:45							
10							
10:15							
10:30							
10:45							
11							
11:15							
11:30							
11:45							
Total Hours:							
1) Planning + Tithing							
2) In Action + Tithing							
3) Personal + Tithing							
4) At Rest + Tithing							

God's Storehouse Principle

MO___ DATE	MON	TUE	WED	THU	FRI	SAT	SUN
12 Noon							
12:15							
12:30							
12:45							
1							
1:15							
1:30							
1:45							
2							
2:15							
2:30							
2:45							
3							
3:15							
3:30							
3:45							
4							
4:15							
4:30							
4:45							
5							
5:15							
5:30							
5:45							
Total Hours:							
1) Personal + Tithing							
2) Planning + Tithing							
3) Working + Tithing							
4) At Rest + Tithing							

© Sheila Holm

MO___ DATE	MON	TUE	WED	THU	FRI	SAT	SUN
6 PM							
6:15							
6:30							
6:45							
7							
7:15							
7:30							
7:45							
8							
8:15							
8:30							
8:45							
9							
9:15							
9:30							
9:45							
10							
10:15							
10:30							
10:45							
11							
11:15							
11:30							
11:45							
Total Hours:							
1) Personal + Tithing							
2) Planning + Tithing							
3) Working + Tithing							
4) At Rest + Tithing							

© Sheila Holm

Each month has an average of 4.33 weeks, after each week, you have the option to insert your life within the hourly format as it becomes clear within this hour by hour version:

MO___ DATE	MON	TUE	WED	THU	FRI	SAT	SUN
12 M							
1							
2							
3							
4							
5							
6							
7							
8							
9							
10							
11							
Noon							
1							
2							
3							
4							
5							
6							
7							
8							
9							
10							
11							
Total Hours:							
1) Personal + Tithing							
2) Planning + Tithing							
3) Working + Tithing							
4) At Rest + Tithing							

WEEK 2

MO___	MON	TUE	WED	THU	FRI	SAT	SUN
DATE							
12 AM							
12:15							
12:30							
12:45							
1							
1:15							
1:30							
1:45							
2							
2:15							
2:30							
2:45							
3							
3:15							
3:30							
3:45							
4							
4:15							
4:30							
4:45							
5							
5:15							
5:30							
5:45							
Total Hours:							
1) Personal + Tithing							
2) Planning + Tithing							
3) Working + Tithing							
4) At Rest + Tithing							

MO___ DATE	MON	TUE	WED	THU	FRI	SAT	SUN
6 AM							
6:15							
6:30							
6:45							
7							
7:15							
7:30							
7:45							
8							
8:15							
8:30							
8:45							
9							
9:15							
9:30							
9:45							
10							
10:15							
10:30							
10:45							
11							
11:15							
11:30							
11:45							
Total Hours:							
1) Planning + Tithing							
2) In Action + Tithing							
3) Personal + Tithing							
4) At Rest + Tithing							

MO___ DATE	MON	TUE	WED	THU	FRI	SAT	SUN
12 Noon							
12:15							
12:30							
12:45							
1							
1:15							
1:30							
1:45							
2							
2:15							
2:30							
2:45							
3							
3:15							
3:30							
3:45							
4							
4:15							
4:30							
4:45							
5							
5:15							
5:30							
5:45							
Total Hours:							
1) Personal + Tithing							
2) Planning + Tithing							
3) Working + Tithing							
4) At Rest + Tithing							

MO___ DATE	MON	TUE	WED	THU	FRI	SAT	SUN
6 PM							
6:15							
6:30							
6:45							
7							
7:15							
7:30							
7:45							
8							
8:15							
8:30							
8:45							
9							
9:15							
9:30							
9:45							
10							
10:15							
10:30							
10:45							
11							
11:15							
11:30							
11:45							
Total Hours:							
1) Personal + Tithing							
2) Planning + Tithing							
3) Working + Tithing							
4) At Rest + Tithing							

Each month has an average of 4.33 weeks, after each week, you have the option to insert your life within the hourly format as it becomes clear within this hour by hour version:

MO___ DATE	MON	TUE	WED	THU	FRI	SAT	SUN
12 M							
1							
2							
3							
4							
5							
6							
7							
8							
9							
10							
11							
Noon							
1							
2							
3							
4							
5							
6							
7							
8							
9							
10							
11							
Total Hours:							
1) Personal + Tithing							
2) Planning + Tithing							
3) Working + Tithing							
4) At Rest + Tithing							

© *Sheila Holm*

91

Week 3

MO___	MON	TUE	WED	THU	FRI	SAT	SUN
DATE							
12 AM							
12:15							
12:30							
12:45							
1							
1:15							
1:30							
1:45							
2							
2:15							
2:30							
2:45							
3							
3:15							
3:30							
3:45							
4							
4:15							
4:30							
4:45							
5							
5:15							
5:30							
5:45							
Total Hours:							
1) Personal + Tithing							
2) Planning + Tithing							
3) Working + Tithing							
4) At Rest + Tithing							

MO___ DATE	MON	TUE	WED	THU	FRI	SAT	SUN
6 AM							
6:15							
6:30							
6:45							
7							
7:15							
7:30							
7:45							
8							
8:15							
8:30							
8:45							
9							
9:15							
9:30							
9:45							
10							
10:15							
10:30							
10:45							
11							
11:15							
11:30							
11:45							
Total Hours:							
1) Planning + Tithing							
2) In Action + Tithing							
3) Personal + Tithing							
4) At Rest + Tithing							

MO___ DATE	MON	TUE	WED	THU	FRI	SAT	SUN
12 Noon							
12:15							
12:30							
12:45							
1							
1:15							
1:30							
1:45							
2							
2:15							
2:30							
2:45							
3							
3:15							
3:30							
3:45							
4							
4:15							
4:30							
4:45							
5							
5:15							
5:30							
5:45							
Total Hours:							
1) Personal + Tithing							
2) Planning + Tithing							
3) Working + Tithing							
4) At Rest + Tithing							

MO___ DATE	MON	TUE	WED	THU	FRI	SAT	SUN
6 PM							
6:15							
6:30							
6:45							
7							
7:15							
7:30							
7:45							
8							
8:15							
8:30							
8:45							
9							
9:15							
9:30							
9:45							
10							
10:15							
10:30							
10:45							
11							
11:15							
11:30							
11:45							
Total Hours:							
1) Personal + Tithing							
2) Planning + Tithing							
3) Working + Tithing							
4) At Rest + Tithing							

© Sheila Holm

Each month has an average of 4.33 weeks, after each week, you have the option to insert your life within the hourly format as it becomes clear within this hour by hour version:

MO___ DATE	MON	TUE	WED	THU	FRI	SAT	SUN
12 M							
1							
2							
3							
4							
5							
6							
7							
8							
9							
10							
11							
Noon							
1							
2							
3							
4							
5							
6							
7							
8							
9							
10							
11							
Total Hours:							
1) Personal + Tithing							
2) Planning + Tithing							
3) Working + Tithing							
4) At Rest + Tithing							

Week 4

MO___	MON	TUE	WED	THU	FRI	SAT	SUN
DATE							
12 AM							
12:15							
12:30							
12:45							
1							
1:15							
1:30							
1:45							
2							
2:15							
2:30							
2:45							
3							
3:15							
3:30							
3:45							
4							
4:15							
4:30							
4:45							
5							
5:15							
5:30							
5:45							
Total Hours:							
1) Personal + Tithing							
2) Planning + Tithing							
3) Working + Tithing							
4) At Rest + Tithing							

MO___ DATE	MON	TUE	WED	THU	FRI	SAT	SUN
6 AM							
6:15							
6:30							
6:45							
7							
7:15							
7:30							
7:45							
8							
8:15							
8:30							
8:45							
9							
9:15							
9:30							
9:45							
10							
10:15							
10:30							
10:45							
11							
11:15							
11:30							
11:45							
Total Hours:							
1) Planning + Tithing							
2) In Action + Tithing							
3) Personal + Tithing							
4) At Rest + Tithing							

MO___ DATE	MON	TUE	WED	THU	FRI	SAT	SUN
12 Noon							
12:15							
12:30							
12:45							
1							
1:15							
1:30							
1:45							
2							
2:15							
2:30							
2:45							
3							
3:15							
3:30							
3:45							
4							
4:15							
4:30							
4:45							
5							
5:15							
5:30							
5:45							
Total Hours:							
1) Personal + Tithing							
2) Planning + Tithing							
3) Working + Tithing							
4) At Rest + Tithing							

© Sheila Holm

MO___ DATE	MON	TUE	WED	THU	FRI	SAT	SUN
6 PM							
6:15							
6:30							
6:45							
7							
7:15							
7:30							
7:45							
8							
8:15							
8:30							
8:45							
9							
9:15							
9:30							
9:45							
10							
10:15							
10:30							
10:45							
11							
11:15							
11:30							
11:45							
Total Hours:							
1) Personal + Tithing							
2) Planning + Tithing							
3) Working + Tithing							
4) At Rest + Tithing							

Each month has an average of 4.33 weeks, after each week, you have the option to insert your life within the hourly format as it becomes clear within this hour by hour version:

MO___ DATE	MON	TUE	WED	THU	FRI	SAT	SUN
12 M							
1							
2							
3							
4							
5							
6							
7							
8							
9							
10							
11							
Noon							
1							
2							
3							
4							
5							
6							
7							
8							
9							
10							
11							
Total Hours:							
1) Personal + Tithing							
2) Planning + Tithing							
3) Working + Tithing							
4) At Rest + Tithing							

Week 5

MO___	MON	TUE	WED	THU	FRI	SAT	SUN
DATE							
12 AM							
12:15							
12:30							
12:45							
1							
1:15							
1:30							
1:45							
2							
2:15							
2:30							
2:45							
3							
3:15							
3:30							
3:45							
4							
4:15							
4:30							
4:45							
5							
5:15							
5:30							
5:45							
Total Hours:							
1) Personal + Tithing							
2) Planning + Tithing							
3) Working + Tithing							
4) At Rest + Tithing							

MO___ DATE	MON	TUE	WED	THU	FRI	SAT	SUN
6 AM							
6:15							
6:30							
6:45							
7							
7:15							
7:30							
7:45							
8							
8:15							
8:30							
8:45							
9							
9:15							
9:30							
9:45							
10							
10:15							
10:30							
10:45							
11							
11:15							
11:30							
11:45							
Total Hours:							
1) Planning + Tithing							
2) In Action + Tithing							
3) Personal + Tithing							
4) At Rest + Tithing							

© Sheila Holm

MO___ DATE	MON	TUE	WED	THU	FRI	SAT	SUN
12 Noon							
12:15							
12:30							
12:45							
1							
1:15							
1:30							
1:45							
2							
2:15							
2:30							
2:45							
3							
3:15							
3:30							
3:45							
4							
4:15							
4:30							
4:45							
5							
5:15							
5:30							
5:45							
Total Hours:							
1) Personal + Tithing							
2) Planning + Tithing							
3) Working + Tithing							
4) At Rest + Tithing							

© *Sheila Holm*

God's Storehouse Principle

MO___ DATE	MON	TUE	WED	THU	FRI	SAT	SUN
6 PM							
6:15							
6:30							
6:45							
7							
7:15							
7:30							
7:45							
8							
8:15							
8:30							
8:45							
9							
9:15							
9:30							
9:45							
10							
10:15							
10:30							
10:45							
11							
11:15							
11:30							
11:45							
Total Hours:							
1) Personal + Tithing							
2) Planning + Tithing							
3) Working + Tithing							
4) At Rest + Tithing							

© Sheila Holm

God's Storehouse Principle

Each month has an average of 4.33 weeks, after each week, you have the option to insert your life within the hourly format as it becomes clear within this hour by hour version:

MO___ DATE	MON	TUE	WED	THU	FRI	SAT	SUN
12 M							
1							
2							
3							
4							
5							
6							
7							
8							
9							
10							
11							
Noon							
1							
2							
3							
4							
5							
6							
7							
8							
9							
10							
11							
Total Hours:							
1) Personal + Tithing							
2) Planning + Tithing							
3) Working + Tithing							
4) At Rest + Tithing							

© Sheila Holm

Third Month of Practice:

Week 1

MO___	MON	TUE	WED	THU	FRI	SAT	SUN
DATE							
12 AM							
12:15							
12:30							
12:45							
1							
1:15							
1:30							
1:45							
2							
2:15							
2:30							
2:45							
3							
3:15							
3:30							
3:45							
4							
4:15							
4:30							
4:45							
5							
5:15							
5:30							
5:45							
Total Hours:							
1) Personal + Tithing							
2) Planning + Tithing							
3) Working + Tithing							
4) At Rest + Tithing							

© Sheila Holm

MO___ DATE	MON	TUE	WED	THU	FRI	SAT	SUN
6 AM							
6:15							
6:30							
6:45							
7							
7:15							
7:30							
7:45							
8							
8:15							
8:30							
8:45							
9							
9:15							
9:30							
9:45							
10							
10:15							
10:30							
10:45							
11							
11:15							
11:30							
11:45							
Total Hours:							
1) Planning + Tithing							
2) In Action + Tithing							
3) Personal + Tithing							
4) At Rest + Tithing							

God's Storehouse Principle

MO___ DATE	MON	TUE	WED	THU	FRI	SAT	SUN
12 Noon							
12:15							
12:30							
12:45							
1							
1:15							
1:30							
1:45							
2							
2:15							
2:30							
2:45							
3							
3:15							
3:30							
3:45							
4							
4:15							
4:30							
4:45							
5							
5:15							
5:30							
5:45							
Total Hours:							
1) Personal + Tithing							
2) Planning + Tithing							
3) Working + Tithing							
4) At Rest + Tithing							

© Sheila Holm

MO___ DATE	MON	TUE	WED	THU	FRI	SAT	SUN
6 PM							
6:15							
6:30							
6:45							
7							
7:15							
7:30							
7:45							
8							
8:15							
8:30							
8:45							
9							
9:15							
9:30							
9:45							
10							
10:15							
10:30							
10:45							
11							
11:15							
11:30							
11:45							
Total Hours:							
1) Personal + Tithing							
2) Planning + Tithing							
3) Working + Tithing							
4) At Rest + Tithing							

Each month has an average of 4.33 weeks, after each week, you have the option to insert your life within the hourly format as it becomes clear within this hour by hour version:

MO___ DATE	MON	TUE	WED	THU	FRI	SAT	SUN
12 M							
1							
2							
3							
4							
5							
6							
7							
8							
9							
10							
11							
Noon							
1							
2							
3							
4							
5							
6							
7							
8							
9							
10							
11							
Total Hours:							
1) P ersonal + Tithing							
2) Planning + Tithing							
3) Working + Tithing							
4) At Rest + Tithing							

WEEK 2

MO___	MON	TUE	WED	THU	FRI	SAT	SUN
DATE							
12 AM							
12:15							
12:30							
12:45							
1							
1:15							
1:30							
1:45							
2							
2:15							
2:30							
2:45							
3							
3:15							
3:30							
3:45							
4							
4:15							
4:30							
4:45							
5							
5:15							
5:30							
5:45							
Total Hours:							
1) Personal + Tithing							
2) Planning + Tithing							
3) Working + Tithing							
4) At Rest + Tithing							

© Sheila Holm

MO___ DATE	MON	TUE	WED	THU	FRI	SAT	SUN
6 AM							
6:15							
6:30							
6:45							
7							
7:15							
7:30							
7:45							
8							
8:15							
8:30							
8:45							
9							
9:15							
9:30							
9:45							
10							
10:15							
10:30							
10:45							
11							
11:15							
11:30							
11:45							
Total Hours:							
1) Planning + Tithing							
2) In Action + Tithing							
3) Personal + Tithing							
4) At Rest + Tithing							

© Sheila Holm

MO___ DATE	MON	TUE	WED	THU	FRI	SAT	SUN
12 Noon							
12:15							
12:30							
12:45							
1							
1:15							
1:30							
1:45							
2							
2:15							
2:30							
2:45							
3							
3:15							
3:30							
3:45							
4							
4:15							
4:30							
4:45							
5							
5:15							
5:30							
5:45							
Total Hours:							
1) Personal + Tithing							
2) Planning + Tithing							
3) Working + Tithing							
4) At Rest + Tithing							

© *Sheila Holm*

MO___ DATE	MON	TUE	WED	THU	FRI	SAT	SUN
6 PM							
6:15							
6:30							
6:45							
7							
7:15							
7:30							
7:45							
8							
8:15							
8:30							
8:45							
9							
9:15							
9:30							
9:45							
10							
10:15							
10:30							
10:45							
11							
11:15							
11:30							
11:45							
Total Hours:							
1) Personal + Tithing							
2) Planning + Tithing							
3) Working + Tithing							
4) At Rest + Tithing							

Each month has an average of 4.33 weeks, after each week, you have the option to insert your life within the hourly format as it becomes clear within this hour by hour version:

MO___ DATE	MON	TUE	WED	THU	FRI	SAT	SUN
12 M							
1							
2							
3							
4							
5							
6							
7							
8							
9							
10							
11							
Noon							
1							
2							
3							
4							
5							
6							
7							
8							
9							
10							
11							
Total Hours:							
1) Personal + Tithing							
2) Planning + Tithing							
3) Working + Tithing							
4) At Rest + Tithing							

Week 3

MO___	MON	TUE	WED	THU	FRI	SAT	SUN
DATE							
12 AM							
12:15							
12:30							
12:45							
1							
1:15							
1:30							
1:45							
2							
2:15							
2:30							
2:45							
3							
3:15							
3:30							
3:45							
4							
4:15							
4:30							
4:45							
5							
5:15							
5:30							
5:45							
Total Hours:							
1) Personal + Tithing							
2) Planning + Tithing							
3) Working + Tithing							
4) At Rest + Tithing							

© Sheila Holm

MO___ DATE	MON	TUE	WED	THU	FRI	SAT	SUN
6 AM							
6:15							
6:30							
6:45							
7							
7:15							
7:30							
7:45							
8							
8:15							
8:30							
8:45							
9							
9:15							
9:30							
9:45							
10							
10:15							
10:30							
10:45							
11							
11:15							
11:30							
11:45							
Total Hours:							
1) Planning + Tithing							
2) In Action + Tithing							
3) Personal + Tithing							
4) At Rest + Tithing							

© Sheila Holm

God's Storehouse Principle

MO___ DATE	MON	TUE	WED	THU	FRI	SAT	SUN
12 Noon							
12:15							
12:30							
12:45							
1							
1:15							
1:30							
1:45							
2							
2:15							
2:30							
2:45							
3							
3:15							
3:30							
3:45							
4							
4:15							
4:30							
4:45							
5							
5:15							
5:30							
5:45							
Total Hours:							
1) Personal + Tithing							
2) Planning + Tithing							
3) Working + Tithing							
4) At Rest + Tithing							

© Sheila Holm

MO___ DATE	MON	TUE	WED	THU	FRI	SAT	SUN
6 PM							
6:15							
6:30							
6:45							
7							
7:15							
7:30							
7:45							
8							
8:15							
8:30							
8:45							
9							
9:15							
9:30							
9:45							
10							
10:15							
10:30							
10:45							
11							
11:15							
11:30							
11:45							
Total Hours:							
1) P ersonal + Tithing							
2) Planning + Tithing							
3) Working + Tithing							
4) At Rest + Tithing							

Each month has an average of 4.33 weeks, after each week, you have the option to insert your life within the hourly format as it becomes clear within this hour by hour version:

MO___ DATE	MON	TUE	WED	THU	FRI	SAT	SUN
12 M							
1							
2							
3							
4							
5							
6							
7							
8							
9							
10							
11							
Noon							
1							
2							
3							
4							
5							
6							
7							
8							
9							
10							
11							
Total Hours:							
1) Personal + Tithing							
2) Planning + Tithing							
3) Working + Tithing							
4) At Rest + Tithing							

Week 4

MO___	MON	TUE	WED	THU	FRI	SAT	SUN
DATE							
12 AM							
12:15							
12:30							
12:45							
1							
1:15							
1:30							
1:45							
2							
2:15							
2:30							
2:45							
3							
3:15							
3:30							
3:45							
4							
4:15							
4:30							
4:45							
5							
5:15							
5:30							
5:45							
Total Hours:							
1) Personal + Tithing							
2) Planning + Tithing							
3) Working + Tithing							
4) At Rest + Tithing							

God's Storehouse Principle

MO___ DATE	MON	TUE	WED	THU	FRI	SAT	SUN
6 AM							
6:15							
6:30							
6:45							
7							
7:15							
7:30							
7:45							
8							
8:15							
8:30							
8:45							
9							
9:15							
9:30							
9:45							
10							
10:15							
10:30							
10:45							
11							
11:15							
11:30							
11:45							
Total Hours:							
1) Planning + Tithing							
2) In Action + Tithing							
3) Personal + Tithing							
4) At Rest + Tithing							

© *Sheila Holm*

MO___ DATE	MON	TUE	WED	THU	FRI	SAT	SUN
12 Noon							
12:15							
12:30							
12:45							
1							
1:15							
1:30							
1:45							
2							
2:15							
2:30							
2:45							
3							
3:15							
3:30							
3:45							
4							
4:15							
4:30							
4:45							
5							
5:15							
5:30							
5:45							
Total Hours:							
1) Personal + Tithing							
2) Planning + Tithing							
3) Working + Tithing							
4) At Rest + Tithing							

© *Sheila Holm*

MO___ DATE	MON	TUE	WED	THU	FRI	SAT	SUN
6 PM							
6:15							
6:30							
6:45							
7							
7:15							
7:30							
7:45							
8							
8:15							
8:30							
8:45							
9							
9:15							
9:30							
9:45							
10							
10:15							
10:30							
10:45							
11							
11:15							
11:30							
11:45							
Total Hours:							
1) Personal + Tithing							
2) Planning + Tithing							
3) Working + Tithing							
4) At Rest + Tithing							

Each month has an average of 4.33 weeks, after each week, you have the option to insert your life within the hourly format as it becomes clear within this hour by hour version:

MO___ DATE	MON	TUE	WED	THU	FRI	SAT	SUN
12 M							
1							
2							
3							
4							
5							
6							
7							
8							
9							
10							
11							
Noon							
1							
2							
3							
4							
5							
6							
7							
8							
9							
10							
11							
Total Hours:							
1) Personal + Tithing							
2) Planning + Tithing							
3) Working + Tithing							
4) At Rest + Tithing							

God's Storehouse Principle

Week 5

MO___	MON	TUE	WED	THU	FRI	SAT	SUN
DATE							
12 AM							
12:15							
12:30							
12:45							
1							
1:15							
1:30							
1:45							
2							
2:15							
2:30							
2:45							
3							
3:15							
3:30							
3:45							
4							
4:15							
4:30							
4:45							
5							
5:15							
5:30							
5:45							
Total Hours:							
1) Personal + Tithing							
2) Planning + Tithing							
3) Working + Tithing							
4) At Rest + Tithing							

© Sheila Holm

MO___ DATE	MON	TUE	WED	THU	FRI	SAT	SUN
6 AM							
6:15							
6:30							
6:45							
7							
7:15							
7:30							
7:45							
8							
8:15							
8:30							
8:45							
9							
9:15							
9:30							
9:45							
10							
10:15							
10:30							
10:45							
11							
11:15							
11:30							
11:45							
Total Hours:							
1) Planning + Tithing							
2) In Action + Tithing							
3) Personal + Tithing							
4) At Rest + Tithing							

MO___ DATE	MON	TUE	WED	THU	FRI	SAT	SUN
12 Noon							
12:15							
12:30							
12:45							
1							
1:15							
1:30							
1:45							
2							
2:15							
2:30							
2:45							
3							
3:15							
3:30							
3:45							
4							
4:15							
4:30							
4:45							
5							
5:15							
5:30							
5:45							
Total Hours:							
1) Personal + Tithing							
2) Planning + Tithing							
3) Working + Tithing							
4) At Rest + Tithing							

© Sheila Holm

MO___ DATE	MON	TUE	WED	THU	FRI	SAT	SUN
6 PM							
6:15							
6:30							
6:45							
7							
7:15							
7:30							
7:45							
8							
8:15							
8:30							
8:45							
9							
9:15							
9:30							
9:45							
10							
10:15							
10:30							
10:45							
11							
11:15							
11:30							
11:45							
Total Hours:							
1) Personal + Tithing							
2) Planning + Tithing							
3) Working + Tithing							
4) At Rest + Tithing							

Each month has an average of 4.33 weeks, after each week, you have the option to insert your life within the hourly format as it becomes clear within this hour by hour version:

MO___ DATE	MON	TUE	WED	THU	FRI	SAT	SUN
12 M							
1							
2							
3							
4							
5							
6							
7							
8							
9							
10							
11							
Noon							
1							
2							
3							
4							
5							
6							
7							
8							
9							
10							
11							
Total Hours:							
1) Personal + Tithing							
2) Planning + Tithing							
3) Working + Tithing							
4) At Rest + Tithing							

© Sheila Holm

This is the first step in 'jumping into the game' of your life. Here's to you, and to your personal success becoming evident to you and to everyone in your life as you begin to participate in **The Balanced Life Game,** based upon **God's Storehouse Principle.**

When you prepared your calendar for this week, did you insert your time with God 1st? If not, quickly go back – remember, God gives 2nd chances!

Did you make your personal time & time with those you hold dear your next priority? If not, quickly go back – remember, God gives 2nd chances!

OK, is the schedule starting to look like you have a life? Great!

The reports are amazing!

One man spent a 15 minute time slot with his teenage son the night of our first meeting. His thought prior to our meeting was 'give him independence' to make his choices and decisions. That night, he found out his son was contemplating suicide that very night due to thinking nobody cared about him since his dad was always busy and tired, unavailable to spend time with him.

One woman decided to give her husband her full attention and tell him what he means to her beginning with a 15 minute time slot. When he revealed he was thinking of divorce since she had become unavailable, God healed them!

Each morning, just pretend God is looking over your shoulder, as you seek time to spend with Him and then for you and for the life you hold precious with those hold most dear! The truth: Soon you will forget you are pretending, because God's wisdom confirms He is with you, looking over your shoulder!!!

Congratulations! Now, live it & pass it on & experience HIS Best! *Sheila*

Chapter 2   Cod's Storehouse Principle   Cash Flow & Pay Off Plan

If you are wondering, ***"How can I pay the debt?"*** Schedule more personal time with God! The plans God has for you are to prosper you!

Viewing all sources of income, the total amounts, as cash entering our life for our purpose and plan to be fulfilled!

The world has 'confused us' by switching credit and debt definitions.

Lie: We are told credit cards limits being increased and increased credit or equity line limits are good. However, everything about credit limits, limits our ability to have good credit Did you know the world downgrades your credit if you spend beyond 50% of the credit limit? Our spending of what they call credit actually equates to increased debt!

Lie: Telling us we are gaining credit, when all credit cards do is to rob / steal / destroy our cash flow. If you do not pay the full amount before the due date, fees will be added. Many credit companies add the fees based upon the date you used your 'credit' on the card or equity line. It is best to not rely on the cards, however, if you want to use them for convenience, check to see if you have cards which do not charge fees from the date of the transaction. Then, before the 'monthly cycle date' check to see if you can pay off the balance without paying fees, otherwise you are paying fees and often high interest to merely have the convenience vs carrying cash to make the purchase.

When I advise people to ONLY use cash for 1-3 month, they find their spending habits change drastically. The 'put in on the card' caused them to overspend and not be able to be 'liquid' each month. When I asked them to merely add up all of the credit card company fees and interest they paid the previous year, they switched transactions to 'all cash' or no credit purchases.

Whether income is a monthly paycheck or two, or multiple sources, it helps to shift all income to appear within a Cash Flow, aka 'Flowing Cash' through your daily life chart so you will see how the cash required is available to fulfill upon the plan for today. It requires a different format to look at cash God's way so you can view CASH IN and where you want to place it vs immediately looking at it as grabbing all of it before it arrives because you have so many places for the cash to go, for the stack of bills to be paid, aka CASH OUT.

CASH IN (from one or multiple sources)

10%   Tithing account

10%   Savings account

_____   Entertainment account

_____   Weekend "get away" account

_____   Vacation account

_____   Contribution account

_____   Tax payment account (property/state/federal)

_____   Retirement plan account

_____   Health benefit (deductible) account

_____   Insurance (auto/home, deductible) account

(add accounts which align with your personal needs)

This structure supports a plan which gives us hope and a future!

Jeremiah 29:11 (NIV)

For I know the plans I have for you," declares the Lord, "plans to prosper you and not to harm you, plans to give you hope and a future.

    CASH OUT (include all costs for each item, within one line item amount)

    ___% Home (Mortgage, Ins., Maint., Taxes, Utilities, Improvements, etc.)

    ___% Auto (Payment, Ins., Maint., DMV & Lic. Fees, Fuel, Wash, etc.)

    ___% Health Care (Insurance, Preventative, Gym, Nutritional, etc.)

    ___% Education (Courses, Books, Training Programs, Seminars, etc.)

    ___% Debt (credit cards, personal loans, additional debt, etc.)

Changing the focus from "paying the monthly bills, per month, each month" with nothing "extra" to show for all of the effort, to establishing a "PAY OFF PLAN."

Cash Flow, Pay Off Plan, requires converting from budgeting the bills, to planning the income flowing through our daily life.

Shifting the bottom line focus / results from the amount of the monthly bills, to the amount of the contribution to lower the entire debt to 'pay off' point. Planning each day to achieve the goal of assets being free and clear, with -0- debt, -0- indebtedness.

Again, since hindsight give us 20/20 vision regarding our finances, assets and debts, it is easier if we back into the Monthly, Weekly, Daily Flow of Cash.

We view the Cash Flow as it CYCLES IN & OUT of our life, as we begin to plan the adjustments required to shift from indebtedness to -0- debt or indebtedness.

Storehouse Principle   **Cash Flow & Pay Off Plan**   **Action Plan**

MONEY Flowing IN (gross amount of income, including taxes withheld if applicable):

Income Sources	Amount	IN	by the 5th, 10th, 15th, 20th, 25th
1. Paycheck or Contract Payment			
2. Residual Income			
3. Paycheck or Contract Payment			
4. Residual Income			
5. Paycheck or Contract Payment			
6. % Investments			
7. % Savings			
8. Personal or Family Income			
9. Personal or Family Business			
10. Sales of Products/Services			

OVER/UNDER BUDGET: _____

MONEY Flowing OUT (gross amount of money to each source, then the monthly amount)

Payment/Planning Sources   Amount OUT by the 5th, 10th, 15th, 20th, 25th

1. Contributions OUT – Community

2. Contributions – Others

3. SAVINGS/RETIREMENT

4. Investments

5. TAXES – withheld or set aside

6. HOUSING
   (incl. Mortgage Payments, Taxes/Ins/Maint/Upgrades)

7. Household EXPENSES related to groceries, utilities, etc.

8. TRANSPORTATION
   (incl. Maint., DMV, Ins/Fuel/Upgrades)

9. Personal EXPENSES personal life, clothing, dry cleaning, trips, etc.

10. 'Pay Off' Plan & Daily/Weekly/Monthly Events & Vacation, etc.

FUTURE PLAN:
     Contributions to Community
     Contributions to Others
     Savings/Retirement
     Investments & "events"

PAY OFF PLAN:
     Taxes
     BALANCE DUE: PAY OFF DATE:
     _____ Mortgage Balance   _____
     _____ Lease/Purchase of Auto Balance   _____
     _____ Balance of Credit Cards for Household Expenses   _____
     _____ Balance of Credit Cards for Personal Expenses   _____
     _____ Balance of Credit Cards for Business Expenses   _____

Monthly: Transfer the fact to the 'Financial Analysis' format and identify Month.

New Cash Flow forms to support the change from indebtedness to -0- debt are provided.

Monthly Financial Analysis   JANUARY Total Sources

Month Income	Income 5th	Income 10th	Income 15th	Income 20th	Income 25th
TOTAL Contributions IN					
Contributions to Community					
Contributions to Others					
Contribution for Taxes					
Cash Available					
Contribution for Future					
TOTAL for Contributions					
Over/Under Budget					
TOTAL					

Contributions OUT to: Total Due Due Now Due 5th Due 10th Due 15th Due 20th Due 25th

1)

2)

3)

4)

5)

6)

7)

TOTAL Contributed to the Community _____

"Pay Down Balance Plan" Dollars Contributed_____

"Future Plan" Dollars Contributed to Savings/Invest _____

© *Sheila Holm*

Monthly Financial Analysis   FEBRUARY Total Sources

Month Income	Income 5th	Income 10th	Income 15th	Income 20th	Income 25th
TOTAL Contributions IN					
Contributions to Community					
Contributions to Others					
Contribution for Taxes					
Cash Available					
Contribution for Future					
TOTAL for Contributions					
Over/Under Budget					
TOTAL					

Contributions OUT to: Total Due Due Now Due 5th Due 10th Due 15th Due 20th Due 25th

1)

2)

3)

4)

5)

6)

7)

TOTAL Contributed to the Community _____

"Pay Down Balance Plan" Dollars Contributed_____

"Future Plan" Dollars Contributed to Savings/Invest _____

© Sheila Holm

Monthly Financial Analysis   MARCH Total Sources

Month Income	Income 5th	Income 10th	Income 15th	Income 20th	Income 25th
TOTAL Contributions IN					
Contributions to Community					
Contributions to Others					
Contribution for Taxes					
Cash Available					
Contribution for Future					
TOTAL for Contributions					
Over/Under Budget					
TOTAL					

Contributions OUT to: Total Due Due Now Due 5th Due 10th Due 15th Due 20th Due 25th

1) _____

2) _____

3) _____

4) _____

5) _____

6) _____

7) _____

TOTAL Contributed to the Community _____

*"Pay Down Balance Plan" Dollars Contributed*_____

"Future Plan" Dollars Contributed to Savings/Invest _____

© Sheila Holm

Monthly Financial Analysis   APRIL Total Sources

Month Income	Income 5th	Income 10th	Income 15th	Income 20th	Income 25th
TOTAL Contributions IN					
Contributions to Community					
Contributions to Others					
Contribution for Taxes					
Cash Available					
Contribution for Future					
TOTAL for Contributions					
Over/Under Budget					
TOTAL					

Contributions OUT to: Total Due   Due Now   Due 5th   Due 10th   Due 15th   Due 20th   Due 25th

1)

2)

3)

4)

5)

6)

7)

TOTAL Contributed to the Community _____

"Pay Down Balance Plan" Dollars Contributed_____

"Future Plan" Dollars Contributed to Savings/Invest _____

© Sheila Holm

Monthly Financial Analysis   MAY Total Sources

Month Income	Income 5th	Income 10th	Income 15th	Income 20th	Income 25th
TOTAL Contributions IN					
Contributions to Community					
Contributions to Others					
Contribution for Taxes					
Cash Available					
Contribution for Future					
TOTAL for Contributions					
Over/Under Budget					
TOTAL					

Contributions OUT to:	Total Due	Due Now	Due 5th	Due 10th	Due 15th	Due 20th	Due 25th
1)							
2)							
3)							
4)							
5)							
6)							
7)							

TOTAL Contributed to the Community _____

"Pay Down Balance Plan" Dollars Contributed_____

"Future Plan" Dollars Contributed to Savings/Invest _____

© *Sheila Holm*

Monthly Financial Analysis   JUNE Total Sources

Month Income	Income 5th	Income 10th	Income 15th	Income 20th	Income 25th
TOTAL Contributions IN					
Contributions to Community					
Contributions to Others					
Contribution for Taxes					
Cash Available					
Contribution for Future					
TOTAL for Contributions					
Over/Under Budget					
TOTAL					

Contributions OUT to: Total Due Due Now Due 5th Due 10th Due 15th Due 20th Due 25th

1)

2)

3)

4)

5)

6)

7)

TOTAL Contributed to the Community _____

"Pay Down Balance Plan" Dollars Contributed_____

"Future Plan" Dollars Contributed to Savings/Invest _____

© Sheila Holm

Monthly Financial Analysis   JULY Total Sources

Month Income	Income 5th	Income 10th	Income 15th	Income 20th	Income 25th
TOTAL Contributions IN					
Contributions to Community					
Contributions to Others					
Contribution for Taxes					
Cash Available					
Contribution for Future					
TOTAL for Contributions					
Over/Under Budget					
TOTAL					

Contributions OUT to: Total Due Due Now   Due 5th   Due 10th   Due 15th   Due 20th   Due 25th

1)

2)

3)

4)

5)

6)

7)

TOTAL Contributed to the Community _____

"Pay Down Balance Plan" Dollars Contributed_____

"Future Plan" Dollars Contributed to Savings/Invest _____

© Sheila Holm

Monthly Financial Analysis

AUGUST Total Sources

Month Income	Income 5th	Income 10th	Income 15th	Income 20th	Income 25th
TOTAL Contributions IN					
Contributions to Community					
Contributions to Others					
Contribution for Taxes					
Cash Available					
Contribution for Future					
TOTAL for Contributions					
Over/Under Budget					
TOTAL					

Contributions OUT to:	Total Due	Due Now	Due 5th	Due 10th	Due 15th	Due 20th	Due 25th
1)							
2)							
3)							
4)							
5)							
6)							
7)							

TOTAL Contributed to the Community _____

"Pay Down Balance Plan" Dollars Contributed_____

"Future Plan" Dollars Contributed to Savings/Invest _____

Monthly Financial Analysis   SEPTEMBER Total Sources

Month Income	Income 5th	Income 10th	Income 15th	Income 20th	Income 25th
TOTAL Contributions IN					
Contributions to Community					
Contributions to Others					
Contribution for Taxes					
Cash Available					
Contribution for Future					
TOTAL for Contributions					
Over/Under Budget					
TOTAL					

Contributions OUT to: Total Due Due Now   Due 5th Due 10th   Due 15th   Due 20th   Due 25th

1)
_____

2)
_____

3)
_____

4)
_____

5)
_____

6)
_____

7)
_____

TOTAL Contributed to the Community _____

"Pay Down Balance Plan" Dollars Contributed_____

"Future Plan" Dollars Contributed to Savings/Invest _____

© *Sheila Holm*

Monthly Financial Analysis — OCTOBER Total Sources

Month Income	Income 5th	Income 10th	Income 15th	Income 20th	Income 25th
TOTAL Contributions IN					
Contributions to Community					
Contributions to Others					
Contribution for Taxes					
Cash Available					
Contribution for Future					
TOTAL for Contributions					
Over/Under Budget					
TOTAL					

Contributions OUT to: Total Due Due Now Due 5th Due 10th Due 15th Due 20th Due 25th

1)

2)

3)

4)

5)

6)

7)

TOTAL Contributed to the Community _____

"Pay Down Balance Plan" Dollars Contributed_____

"Future Plan" Dollars Contributed to Savings/Invest _____

Monthly Financial Analysis   NOVEMBER Total Sources

Month Income	Income 5th	Income 10th	Income 15th	Income 20th	Income 25th
TOTAL Contributions IN					
Contributions to Community					
Contributions to Others					
Contribution for Taxes					
Cash Available					
Contribution for Future					
TOTAL for Contributions					
Over/Under Budget					
TOTAL					

Contributions OUT to: Total Due Due Now   Due 5th Due 10th   Due 15th   Due 20th   Due 25th

1)

2)

3)

4)

5)

6)

7)

TOTAL Contributed to the Community _____

"Pay Down Balance Plan" Dollars Contributed_____

"Future Plan" Dollars Contributed to Savings/Invest _____

© Sheila Holm

Monthly Financial Analysis   DECEMBER Total Sources

Month Income	Income 5th	Income 10th	Income 15th	Income 20th	Income 25th
TOTAL Contributions IN					
Contributions to Community					
Contributions to Others					
Contribution for Taxes					
Cash Available					
Contribution for Future					
TOTAL for Contributions					
Over/Under Budget					
TOTAL					

Contributions OUT to:	Total Due	Due Now	Due 5th	Due 10th	Due 15th	Due 20th	Due 25th
1)							
2)							
3)							
4)							
5)							
6)							
7)							

TOTAL Contributed to the Community _____

"Pay Down Balance Plan" Dollars Contributed_____

"Future Plan" Dollars Contributed to Savings/Invest _____

© *Sheila Holm*

MILLION DOLLAR GAME

In our lifetime, we actually handle a million dollars, or two or more.

At $20,000 per year, it would take 50 years to earn our million, and at $50,000 per year, it would only take 20 years, without one increase in pay!

A plan should be in place to confirm how we will benefit the most from our million(s). This is why the million dollar game is established, once we know how to proceed with a cash flow vs. a budget the bills plan.

Focusing upon our personal $1,000,000 plan changes our perspective for each purchase decision and each dollar we spend.

Overall plan for our cash flow to represent something in life vs. copies of bills paid is confirmed within the MILLION DOLLAR GAME.

The game supports focusing upon how to pay off our home, vacation home, auto(s), and all of the indebtedness in life, to LIVE a BALANCED 'Extra' ordinary LIFE!

MILLION DOLLAR GAME is played per the workbook outline:

MILLION dollar life:	Dollars	Remaining Dollars
Begin with 1st MILLION DOLLARS ...	$1,000,000	
Then, "pay off" plan to "pay off" the house(s)	_____	
Then, "pay off" plan to "pay off" the auto(s)	_____	
Then, "pay off" plan to "pay off" the credit cards:		
Household	_____	
Personal	_____	
Business	_____	
Then, "pay off" plan for vacations/events	_____	
And "pay off" plan for vacation/retirement home	_____	
BALANCE:		_____
Then, the Contribution to the Community	_____	
What will be "in the community" because you lived?	_____	
Then, "set aside" for your savings/future	_____	
How will your savings impact the future?	_____	
Then, ___% tax dollars to be "set aside"	_____	
BALANCE:		_____

Chapter 3   Storehouse Principle   Planning

Failing to plan is actually planning to fail.

1 requirement for planning: Schedule time to plan!

2 requirement to plan: Establish a plan!

3 requirement for the plan: Proceed upon a viable, workable, life plan!

GOALS FOR TODAY:

'To Do' list of each of the DAILY DETAILS

Random lists of activities and tasks are OK, since it is more important to include each activity and task as you think of it, so you are sure that each one is on the list!

Planning process is the next step, while it is important to remember: more and more tasks and activities will be added, as each hour of the day unfolds and the week progresses.

You can begin with a blank piece of paper while the form in the workbook includes options to remain 'flexible' while making the list. This is done to support your personal "flexible" cooperation!

RESULT: Quickly prioritize the variety of activities and tasks to be completed today, and/or another day in the week/month, when an item is not a top priority for today. Within the workbook, the form helps accomplishing the tasks and activities during the day, the week, and/or the month.

Blank paper or on the form provided, the page(s) are not rewritten as each item is completed. It is 'checked off of the list' when 'it is finished' since each of the many activities and tasks added during the day / week / month shift the original priorities.

PROCESS: Topics on the list. Scroll down the list and select the most important items and write # 1 in front of no more than five items. Prioritizing the items with # 2 on the next five, # 3 on the next five and so on will help keep the plans in perspective, until you have prioritized each of the items.

When you add items and/or pages, as the hours of the day and days of the week progress, you will need to take a few moments to review the items, and to prioritize them and/or re-prioritize the remaining items on your list.

This process becomes easier each time to begin a new list. When you complete each item, put a heavy line through it and a check mark on the right. On the form, I title that column 'it is finished.'

When each item is checked off of the list, and the appointments are complete, the page can be filed with your daily, weekly and month plans, until the end of the month.

Regarding: Cash Flow plans. The weekend getaways, etc., need to appear within the details of your plan! Items requiring attention for the monthly event, a special weekend or an event during the week, need to be included and prioritized with your tasks and activities.

GOALS FOR THIS WEEK:

Summarize the key tasks and activities from the "to do" list, the goals for each day, and include the events planned or special plans made for each day of the week.

'Insert' the working time, the key points of the day and the week, the goals and accomplishments planned for the week, and the personal time, the planning time, and, of course, the hours proceeding upon the goals and activities, and the hours of rest!

ADD:

Weekly financial goals based upon the 5th, the 10th, the 15th, the 20th, the 25th.

NOTE the TOP Financial Plans for: Personal / Family / Business Goals, Monthly Events, Trips, Vacation, etc., with:

Weekly Schedule of Contributions to _____

Contributions to Personal / Business Plans _____

Contributions to remaining bills, etc. _____

Actual Dollars Available _____

Dollars 'set aside' for current or future Event(s) _____

NOTE the TOP Plans, People & Resources:

TOP - Plans for Personal LIFE

TOP - 'Planning' items in daily/weekly/monthly LIFE

TOP – Action ('In Action') items in daily/weekly/monthly LIFE

TOP - People in daily / weekly / monthly LIFE

TOP - Resources in daily / weekly / monthly LIFE

TOP - Plans for Business LIFE

TOP - 'Planning' items in daily/weekly/monthly LIFE

TOP – Action ('In Action') items in daily/weekly/monthly LIFE

TOP - People in daily / weekly / monthly LIFE

TOP - Resources in daily / weekly / monthly LIFE

GOALS FOR THIS MONTH:

'To Do' Summary of LIFE PLAN key points for the Month.

OVERVIEW of the Monthly Plan, including TOP daily, weekly and monthly plans, events, people to meet with and share time and projects with, and the key points of the month, including the top activities and tasks for the Month.

Monthly PLAN, summarizing the Daily Goals & Weekly Plans:

TOP Financial Plans for:

TOP - 'Planning' items in monthly LIFE

TOP – Action ('In Action') items in monthly LIFE

TOP - People in monthly LIFE

TOP - Resources in monthly LIFE

Planning for Today, This Week, This Month:

Actions to be taken Today & This week   Today's Date: _____ Week of _____ Month: _____

Life/Business Planning:

                                      Project goal _____

                                              (T) Goal for Today _____

                                                      (W) Goal for this Week _____

                                                              (M) Goal for this Month _____

Goal	Priority	Action Plan (call, letter, appointment; items to arrange)	IT IS FINISHED!
T W M	1 2 3		
T W M	1 2 3		
T W M	1 2 3		
T W M	1 2 3		
T W M	1 2 3		
T W M	1 2 3		
T W M	1 2 3		
T W M	1 2 3		
T W M	1 2 3		
T W M	1 2 3		
T W M	1 2 3		
T W M	1 2 3		
T W M	1 2 3		
T W M	1 2 3		
T W M	1 2 3		
T W M	1 2 3		
T W M	1 2 3		
T W M	1 2 3		
T W M	1 2 3		
T W M	1 2 3		
T W M	1 2 3		

Planning for Today, This Week, This Month:

Actions to be taken Today & This week   *Today's Date:* _____ *Week of* _____ *Month:* _____

Life/Business Planning:

Project goal _____
(T) Goal for Today _____
(W) Goal for this Week _____
(M) Goal for this Month _____

Goal	Priority	Action Plan (call, letter, appointment; items to arrange)	IT IS FINISHED!
T W M	1 2 3		
T W M	1 2 3		
T W M	1 2 3		
T W M	1 2 3		
T W M	1 2 3		
T W M	1 2 3		
T W M	1 2 3		
T W M	1 2 3		
T W M	1 2 3		
T W M	1 2 3		
T W M	1 2 3		
T W M	1 2 3		
T W M	1 2 3		
T W M	1 2 3		
T W M	1 2 3		
T W M	1 2 3		
T W M	1 2 3		
T W M	1 2 3		
T W M	1 2 3		
T W M	1 2 3		
T W M	1 2 3		
T W M	1 2 3		

Planning for Today, This Week, This Month:

Actions to be taken Today & This week   Today's Date: _____ Week of _____ Month: _____

Life/Business Planning:

Project goal _____
(T) Goal for Today _____
(W) Goal for this Week _____
(M) Goal for this Month _____

Goal	Priority	Action Plan (call, letter, appointment; items to arrange)	IT IS FINISHED!
T W M	1 2 3		
T W M	1 2 3		
T W M	1 2 3		
T W M	1 2 3		
T W M	1 2 3		
T W M	1 2 3		
T W M	1 2 3		
T W M	1 2 3		
T W M	1 2 3		
T W M	1 2 3		
T W M	1 2 3		
T W M	1 2 3		
T W M	1 2 3		
T W M	1 2 3		
T W M	1 2 3		
T W M	1 2 3		
T W M	1 2 3		
T W M	1 2 3		
T W M	1 2 3		
T W M	1 2 3		
T W M	1 2 3		

Chapter 4   Storehouse Principle   ***Talents, Skills and Abilities***

Life is filled with talents, skills, abilities and resources.

1 - Recognizing our ability, and the ability of the other people in our family and our life, and in our business and industry to make a contribution

2 - Making a contribution, individually, together with family, with other people in our life, including professional colleagues, within our business and industry

List of Talents, Skills and Abilities:

Natural Talents:	Trained Talents:
1.	1.
2.	2.
3.	3.

Natural Skills:	Trained Skills:
1.	1.
2.	2.
3.	3.

Natural Abilities:	Trained Abilities:
1.	1.
2.	2.
3.	3.

List of Training:

Schools	Courses
1.	1.
2.	2.
3.	3.

Seminars	Certificates
1.	1.
2.	2.
3.	3.

Summary of TIME devoted to contributing natural talents, skills and abilities:

Daily   (within the calendar)

Weekly   (within the calendar)

Monthly   (within the calendar)

Summary of MONEY invested in training to improve talents, skills and abilities:

Daily

1.	1.
2.	2.
3.	3.
4.	4.
5.	5.
6.	6.
7.	7.

Weekly (4.3 weeks within a month)

1.

2.

3.

4.

5.

Monthly

1.

2.

3.

4.

5.

6.

7.

8.

9.

10.

11.

12.

People who would benefit from these Talents, Skills and Abilities:

1.

2.

3.

4.

5.

6.

7.

8.

9.

10.

11.

12.

These people become the twelve people to begin discipling!

Congratulations!

CHAPTER 5 Storehouse Principle   People, Networking, Resources

Proceeding step by step, ***Networking through Six Degrees of Separation***

PEOPLE   '*Six Degrees of Separation'*

List three to seven people that are in your life, communicating with you:

PEOPLE – 'involved' in your LIFE, each day, every day, inner circle:

1.

2.

3.

4.

5.

6.

7.

PEOPLE – "involved" in your LIFE, during your business day, next circle:

1.

2.

3.

4.

5.

6.

7.

PEOPLE – 'involved' in your LIFE, during the week, next circle:

1.

2.

3.

4.

5.

6.

7.

PEOPLE – 'involved' in your life, during the weekends, next circle:

1.

2.

3.

4.

5.

6.

7.

PEOPLE – 'involved' in your life, on a monthly basis, next circle:

1.

2.

3.

4.

5.

6.

7.

PEOPLE – 'involved' in your life, occasionally during the year, next circle:

1.

2.

3.

4.

5.

6.

7.

PEOPLE – 'involved' in your life, less frequently, next circle:

1.

2.

3.

4.

5.

6.

7.

PEOPLE – 'additional' people in your life, 'hearing details', next circle:

1.

2.

3.

4.

5.

6.

7.

Now, the truth becomes evident in the process.

1. Put a check mark next to each person knowledgeable of your dreams, goals and LIFE plans.

2. Put a circle next to each person you need to inform about your dreams, goals and LIFE plans:

3. Put an X next to each person supporting your dreams, goals and LIFE plans 100%:

4. Put an * next to each person questioning each decision you make:

LIST (on your planning page and then, within your calendar):

1. All people with a check mark and an X, and add each of their names on separate days of your monthly calendar, with the intention to call, email or communicate with each person.

2. All people with a circle and an X; be sure to inform them of your dreams, goals and LIFE plans.

3. All people with a circle need to hear about your specific dreams, goals and LIFE plans, so they can support or question you about your dreams, goals and LIFE plans.

4. All people with a circle and an *; identify the plans they are not aware of, and then decide if the person should know more about your plans or less about your life and any of your plans.

5. All people with an * need to be identified and a decision needs to be made regarding identifying and discussing the negative impact they may have upon your personal and/or business life, and how often you want to be in communication with them prior to discipling them and / or if God confirms you need to dust off your shoes and discontinue regular contact with them.

REPEAT the above for LIFE & Business Resources: vendors, clients, staff, employees, peers, supervisors, commuters, etc., etc., etc., to be sure all people are included.

PHASE 1:

Identifying the people that influence our life from each 'level / circle' of life, the people 'at the core' of daily life, from the inner circle to the people seven levels out from the inner circle. These people and the people they are networked with make up your six degrees of separation that connects you to everyone.

PHASE 2:

Identifying the top three or four people in each level, and the <u>three</u> to <u>four</u> topic(s) of conversations from two categories:

      1. Tasks, concerns, problems, or issues you are facing in your life,

      2. Plans or goal(s) that are important to you and to your life plan.

NOTE: Additional topics can be identified, while it is best to not list more than seven at this time. Goal: top three!

The top three or four topics in each category should be addressed first.

Then, the next three or four topics can be addressed in the same format.

PHASE 3:

Beginning with the # 1 topic of tasks, concerns, problems or issues:

'Y' for YES by each # 1 next to the name of each person, if the topic has been discussed.

'N' for NO by each # 1 next to the name of each person, if you have not discussed the topic.

'?' by each # 1 next to the name of each person, if you think the person is aware of the topic, however, you are not sure if you have discussed the topic.

Continuing the process until the list is complete for # 1, then for # 2, and # 3, and # 4 topic.

Then, begin with the # 1 topic of plans/goals, and repeat the same process, and then, with # 2, # 3, and # 4.

Part 1: Circle all 'N' topics, and transfer the information onto the 'N' page, noting only the people with 'N' marks identified, and then proceed to the next phase.

Part 2: Circle all '?' topics, and transfer the information onto the '?' page, noting only the people with the '?' marks identified, and proceed to the next phase.

PHASE 4:

After the people on the 'N or the '?' lists are identified, select the people to schedule some time with, to discuss the topic or plans identified.

Add the names and phone numbers to the 'To Do' list and prioritize the time on the 24 hour calendar based upon the same process as the items are scheduled within the TIME section of the workbook.

PERSONAL RESOURCES:

Family and friends in the same industry:

People in the same industry:

Family and friends in the same position:

People in the same position:

People in the same company, in the same position:

Business or professional associations for the position:

Professional resource people for the position:

Training seminars, centers, colleges, etc., for the position:

BUSINESS RESOURCES:

Businesses in the same industry, in the community:

Businesses in the same industry, in the country:

Businesses in the same industry, in the world:

Business or professional organizations established for the industry:

Training seminars, centers, colleges, etc., established for the industry:

TIME & MONEY planned and/or invested in PERSONAL RESOURCES:

TIME & MONEY planned and/or invested in BUSINESS RESOURCES:

NOTE: Sometimes it may seem like we need to replace everyone in our life, while it is critical to remember our lessons in life are typically for our benefit and the opportunity to learn may be based upon discipling the 'problem' people.

CHAPTER 6 Storehouse Principle   Balanced Life Game

Balanced Life Game

PERSONAL LIFE GAME

ONLY Three TOP items to focus on during this day:

Personal LIFE items/plans to focus on

     1.

     2.

     3.

Intimate Relationship LIFE items/plans to focus on

     1.

     2.

     3.

Family & Friend items/plans to focus on

     1.

     2.

     3.

Daily LIFE plan items/plans to focus on

     1.

     2.

     3.

BUSINESS LIFE GAME

ONLY Three TOP items to focus on during this day:

Management LIFE items / plans to focus on: Time/Money/Resources

1.

2.

3.

Financial LIFE items/plans to focus on

1.

2.

3.

Marketing items/plans to focus on

1.

2.

3.

Daily Business LIFE items/plans

1.

2.

3.

PERSONAL & BUSINESS LIFE GAME

ONLY Three TOP items to focus on during this day:

Personal LIFE & Management LIFE items/plans to focus on:

1.

2.

3.

Intimate Relationship & Financial LIFE items/plans to focus on:

1.

2.

3.

Family & Friends & Marketing items/plans to focus on:

1.

2.

3.

Daily LIFE & Business LIFE items/plans to focus on:

1.

2.

3.

EACH GAME BOARD:

Decide:

Between each of the categories.

Are you "IN" or "OUT" of balance?

Rank: (is your life currently a 1 or closer to a 10)

Personal, from 1-10

Business, from 1-10, and

Combined Personal / Business LIFE, from a 1 to 10.

Game boards for each are provided on one page. After the process works well for the Personal and Business boards (usually takes a week or two to grasp the concept and see the flow, so a full week of game boards are inserted for each of the three options). Soon, the combined board is all you need to prepare in the morning.

Easy to complete the boards, confirming your plan for the day within three to five minutes each morning, are provided within the workbook.

Ready? Practice as though your LIFE depended upon it!

And remember: THIS IS YOUR LIFE, SO ENJOY THE GAME!

SATURDAY   **PERSONAL LIFE GAME**

ONLY   Three TOP items to focus on during this day:

Personal LIFE items/plans to focus on

IN   IN

OUT   OUT

ONLY   Three TOP items to focus on: ONLY   Three TOP items to focus on:

Daily LIFE plan   Family & Friend items/plans

DAILY

RANKING

_____

ONLY   Three TOP items to focus on:

Intimate Relationship LIFE items/plan

IN   IN

OUT   OUT

SUNDAY   **PERSONAL LIFE GAME**

ONLY   Three TOP items to focus on during this day:

Personal LIFE items/plans to focus on

IN

OUT

IN

OUT

ONLY   Three TOP items to focus on:

Daily LIFE plan

DAILY

RANKING

ONLY   Three TOP items to focus on:

Family & Friend items/plans

_____

ONLY   Three TOP items to focus on:

Intimate Relationship LIFE items/plan

IN

OUT

IN

OUT

MONDAY   **PERSONAL LIFE GAME**

ONLY   Three TOP items to focus on during this day:

Personal LIFE items/plans to focus on

IN   IN

OUT   OUT

ONLY   Three TOP items to focus on: ONLY   Three TOP items to focus on:

Daily LIFE plan   Family & Friend items/plans

DAILY

RANKING

_____

ONLY   Three TOP items to focus on:

Intimate Relationship LIFE items/plan

IN   IN

OUT   OUT

TUESDAY   **PERSONAL LIFE GAME**

ONLY   Three TOP items to focus on during this day:

Personal LIFE items/plans to focus on

IN   IN

OUT   OUT

ONLY   Three TOP items to focus on: ONLY   Three TOP items to focus on:

Daily LIFE plan   Family & Friend items/plans

DAILY

RANKING

_____

ONLY   Three TOP items to focus on:

Intimate Relationship LIFE items/plan

IN   IN

OUT   OUT

WEDNESDAY   **PERSONAL LIFE GAME**

ONLY   Three TOP items to focus on during this day:

Personal LIFE items/plans to focus on

IN   IN

OUT   OUT

ONLY   Three TOP items to focus on: ONLY   Three TOP items to focus on:

Daily LIFE plan   Family & Friend items/plans

DAILY

RANKING

_____

ONLY   Three TOP items to focus on:

Intimate Relationship LIFE items/plan

IN   IN

OUT   OUT

THURSDAY   **PERSONAL LIFE GAME**

ONLY   Three TOP items to focus on during this day:

Personal LIFE items/plans to focus on

IN   IN

OUT   OUT

ONLY   Three TOP items to focus on: ONLY   Three TOP items to focus on:

Daily LIFE plan   Family & Friend items/plans

DAILY

RANKING

_____

ONLY   Three TOP items to focus on:

Intimate Relationship LIFE items/plan

IN   IN

OUT   OUT

FRIDAY   **PERSONAL LIFE GAME**

ONLY   Three TOP items to focus on during this day:

Personal LIFE items/plans to focus on

IN   IN

OUT   OUT

ONLY   Three TOP items to focus on: ONLY   Three TOP items to focus on:

Daily LIFE plan   Family & Friend items/plans

                              DAILY

                              RANKING

                              _____

ONLY   Three TOP items to focus on:

Intimate Relationship LIFE items/plan

IN   IN

OUT   OUT

SATURDAY   **BUSINESS LIFE GAME**

ONLY   Three TOP items to focus on during this day:

Management LIFE items/plans to focus on: Time/Money/Resources

IN   IN

OUT   OUT

ONLY   Three TOP items to focus on: ONLY   Three TOP items to focus on:

Daily Business LIFE items/plans   Marketing items/plans

DAILY

RANKING

1 to 10:

_____

ONLY   Three TOP items to focus on:

Financial LIFE items/plans

IN   IN

OUT   OUT

SUNDAY   **BUSINESS LIFE GAME**

ONLY   Three TOP items to focus on during this day:

Management LIFE items/plans to focus on: Time/Money/Resources

IN   IN

OUT   OUT

ONLY   Three TOP items to focus on: ONLY   Three TOP items to focus on:

Daily Business LIFE items/plans   Marketing items/plans

DAILY

RANKING

1 to 10:

_____

ONLY   Three TOP items to focus on:

Financial LIFE items/plans

IN   IN

OUT   OUT

God's Storehouse Principle

BUSINESS LIFE GAME

ONLY   Three TOP items to focus on during this day:

Management LIFE items/plans to focus on: Time/Money/Resources

IN   IN

OUT   OUT

ONLY   Three TOP items to focus on: ONLY   Three TOP items to focus on:

Daily Business LIFE items/plans   Marketing items/plans

DAILY

RANKING

1 to 10:

_____

ONLY   Three TOP items to focus on:

Financial LIFE items/plans

IN   IN

OUT   OUT

God's Storehouse Principle

TUESDAY   **BUSINESS LIFE GAME**

ONLY   Three TOP items to focus on during this day:

Management LIFE items/plans to focus on: Time/Money/Resources

IN   IN

OUT   OUT

ONLY   Three TOP items to focus on: ONLY   Three TOP items to focus on:

Daily Business LIFE items/plans   Marketing items/plans

DAILY

RANKING

1 to 10:

———

ONLY   Three TOP items to focus on:

Financial LIFE items/plans

IN   IN

OUT   OUT

WEDNESDAY   **BUSINESS LIFE GAME**

ONLY   Three TOP items to focus on during this day:

Management LIFE items/plans to focus on: Time/Money/Resources

IN   IN

OUT   OUT

ONLY   Three TOP items to focus on:

Daily Business LIFE items/plans

DAILY

RANKING

1 to 10:

_____

ONLY   Three TOP items to focus on:

Marketing items/plans

ONLY   Three TOP items to focus on:

Financial LIFE items/plans

IN   IN

OUT   OUT

THURSDAY   **BUSINESS LIFE GAME**

ONLY   Three TOP items to focus on during this day:

Management LIFE items/plans to focus on: Time/Money/Resources

IN   IN

OUT   OUT

ONLY   Three TOP items to focus on: ONLY   Three TOP items to focus on:

Daily Business LIFE items/plans   Marketing items/plans

DAILY

RANKING

1 to 10:

_____

ONLY   Three TOP items to focus on:

Financial LIFE items/plans

IN   IN

OUT   OUT

FRIDAY   **BUSINESS LIFE GAME**

ONLY   Three TOP items to focus on during this day:

Management LIFE items/plans to focus on: Time/Money/Resources

IN   IN

OUT   OUT

ONLY   Three TOP items to focus on: ONLY   Three TOP items to focus on:

Daily Business LIFE items/plans   Marketing items/plans

DAILY

RANKING

1 to 10:

_____

ONLY   Three TOP items to focus on:

Financial LIFE items/plans

IN   IN

OUT   OUT

SATURDAY **PERSONAL & BUSINESS LIFE GAME**

ONLY   Three TOP items to focus on during this day:

Personal LIFE & Management LIFE items/plans to focus on

IN

OUT

IN

OUT

ONLY   Three TOP items to focus on:

Daily LIFE & Business LIFE items/plans

DAILY

RANKING

_____

ONLY   Three TOP items to focus on:

Family & Friends/Marketing items/plans

ONLY   Three TOP items to focus on:

Intimate Relationship & Financial LIFE items/plans

IN

OUT

IN

OUT

SUNDAY   **PERSONAL & BUSINESS LIFE GAME**

ONLY   Three TOP items to focus on during this day:

Personal LIFE & Management LIFE items/plans to focus on

IN   IN

OUT   OUT

ONLY   Three TOP items to focus on: ONLY   Three TOP items to focus on:

Daily LIFE & Business LIFE items/plans   Family & Friends/Marketing items/plans

DAILY

RANKING

_____

ONLY   Three TOP items to focus on:

Intimate Relationship & Financial LIFE items/plans

IN   IN

OUT   OUT

God's Storehouse Principle

MONDAY   **PERSONAL & BUSINESS LIFE GAME**

ONLY   Three TOP items to focus on during this day:

Personal LIFE & Management LIFE items/plans to focus on

IN   IN

OUT   OUT

ONLY   Three TOP items to focus on: ONLY   Three TOP items to focus on:

Daily LIFE & Business LIFE items/plans   Family & Friends/Marketing items/plans

DAILY

RANKING

_____

ONLY   Three TOP items to focus on:

Intimate Relationship & Financial LIFE items/plans

IN   IN

OUT   OUT

TUESDAY   **PERSONAL & BUSINESS LIFE GAME**

ONLY   Three TOP items to focus on during this day:

Personal LIFE & Management LIFE items/plans to focus on

IN   IN

OUT   OUT

ONLY   Three TOP items to focus on: ONLY   Three TOP items to focus on:

Daily LIFE & Business LIFE items/plans   Family & Friends/Marketing items/plans

DAILY

RANKING

_____

ONLY   Three TOP items to focus on:

Intimate Relationship & Financial LIFE items/plans

IN   IN

OUT   OUT

WEDNESDAY **PERSONAL & BUSINESS LIFE GAME**

ONLY   Three TOP items to focus on during this day:

Personal LIFE & Management LIFE items/plans to focus on

IN   IN

OUT   OUT

ONLY   Three TOP items to focus on: ONLY   Three TOP items to focus on:

Daily LIFE & Business LIFE items/plans   Family & Friends/Marketing items/plans

DAILY

RANKING

_____

ONLY   Three TOP items to focus on:

Intimate Relationship & Financial LIFE items/plans

IN   IN

OUT   OUT

THURSDAY   **PERSONAL & BUSINESS LIFE GAME**

ONLY   Three TOP items to focus on during this day:

Personal LIFE & Management LIFE items/plans to focus on

IN

OUT

IN

OUT

ONLY   Three TOP items to focus on:

Daily LIFE & Business LIFE items/plans

DAILY

RANKING

ONLY   Three TOP items to focus on:

Family & Friends/Marketing items/plans

_____

ONLY   Three TOP items to focus on:

Intimate Relationship & Financial LIFE items/plans

IN

OUT

IN

OUT

God's Storehouse Principle

FRIDAY   **PERSONAL & BUSINESS LIFE GAME**

ONLY   Three TOP items to focus on during this day:

Personal LIFE & Management LIFE items/plans to focus on

IN   IN

OUT   OUT

ONLY   Three TOP items to focus on: ONLY   Three TOP items to focus on:

Daily LIFE & Business LIFE items/plans   Family & Friends/Marketing items/plans

DAILY

RANKING

_____

ONLY   Three TOP items to focus on:

Intimate Relationship & Financial LIFE items/plans

IN   IN

OUT   OUT

God's Storehouse Principle walks us through the daily process to quickly produce a clear, concise, workable plan for your daily life! The result is a plan that is easy to change and adjust as your plans change, minute to minute, during the day. Bottom line: Get into the game and live an "extra" ordinary balanced life!

Results in: Balanced Life Game which begins when we shift our perspective on time, to a 24/7 personal daily focus vs. the world based 8-12 hour calendar day, with half days or no days represented for Saturday or Sunday. A 24 hour/7 day calendar, includes the time required for planning time, which can easily be identified within a full 24/7 life schedule represented each day of the week.

Each chapter, Time, Cash Flow, Pay Off Play and Million Dollar Game, Planning and Resourcing our Talents, Skills, Abilities and Resources, Networking Through Six Degrees of Separation, and Planning, resulting in 'Living the 24/7 Balanced Life Game: Personal, Business and Combined,' while the training shared walks you through the process and provides the tools, techniques, and forms required, since they do not exist in the marketplace, today. The support is provided to help you shift from the current, limited forms and ordinary life, to enjoying 'extra' moments, cash, resources, networking resources and planning options within each of the areas of our life, to live an 'extra' ordinary life.

This is the first step in 'jumping into the game of life.' Here's to you, and to your personal success becoming evident to you and to everyone in your life as you begin to participate in ***The Balanced Life Game*** which is based upon ***God's Storehouse Principle.***

I have faith in your abilities! God does, too!

The good news:

God gives us a new day, every day,

and an entire lifetime to LIVE and complete the plan!

Each morning, just for fun, pretend God is looking over your shoulder as you seek time to spend with him and then the time to devote to your life and the life moments which are precious when they are spent with those hold most dear!

The truth: Soon you will forget you are pretending because God is really with you, looking over your shoulder!!!

Congratulations!

Now, live it & pass it on & expand your inner circle so **all** around about you will also experience HIS Best!

Sheila

Chapter 7   Storehouse Principle   Discipleship and New Assignments

Keep On Discipling!

Discipleship and New Assignments

God's Daily Plan:

Discipleship

Accept new assignments

1.

2.

3.

4.

5.

6.

7.

8.

9.

10.

God's Storehouse Principle:

Keep On Seeding / Harvesting!

Reality Check: Realignment with God's Storehouse Principle

Planning/Preparing (your topic)

1.

2.

3.

Seeding/Nurturing

Harvesting/Storing

Replenishing/Planning

1.

2.

3.

(cycle begins, again)

Planning/Preparing (your topic

1.

2.

3.

Seeding/Nurturing

Harvesting/Storing

Replenishing/Planning

1.

2.

3.

(cycle begins, again)

Planning/Preparing (your topic)

1.

2.

3.

Seeding/Nurturing

Harvesting/Storing

Replenishing/Planning

1.

2.

3.

(cycle begins, again)

Planning/Preparing (your topic)

1.

2.

3.

Seeding/Nurturing

Harvesting/Storing

Replenishing/Planning

1.

2.

3.

(cycle begins, again)

Planning/Preparing (your topic)

1.

2.

3.

Seeding/Nurturing

Harvesting/Storing

Replenishing/Planning

1.

2.

3.

(cycle begins, again)

Planning/Preparing (your topic)

1.

2.

3.

Seeding/Nurturing

Harvesting/Storing

Replenishing/Planning

1.

2.

3.

(cycle begins, again)

My Commitment

My commitment to you in this moment is the same commitment I make to each person attending the seminars and conferences around the world, and to all of the people in churches where I'm invited to preach: I'm here for you, standing firm with you, in truth, for we shall become 'more than conquerors' Romans 8:37 Power and authority multiples when we align with God, and come together to fulfill upon His purpose and plan for these days! **Personal request:** Find one person each day to share God's secret with! Enjoy seeking out seven new people per week. One per day. That's all I ask.

My Prayer for Us

Each time you read these words they will have a deeper impact upon your life, your family / lineage and your sphere of influence in your family, circle of friends and colleagues in your church, business, industry and community, while it blesses you as much each time you read the words as it did the very first time for God's truth holds gems which we discover the deeper we enter into relationship with Him.

Isaiah 40:31 (NIV)

...but those who hope in the LORD will renew their strength. They will soar on wings like eagles; they will run and not grow weary, they will walk and not be faint.

May it be well with your soul in this hour, in these days, while you find 'extra' time to be with God, to bless your life, and to bless all in need of your time, skills, talents, abilities, resources and all God has seeded in you!

May your heart and mind open up to God's 360 degree viewpoint vs. our 'human limited' 90 to 180 degrees 'off course' thinking!

May you realize options for blessing others and find that our 'more than enough' God has granted 'more than enough' time for us to begin to share blessings: time, income, planning options, people, resources, skills, talents and abilities. May we always find ways to share who we are with others, as God directs us to disciple and to be discipled for all of our days of our LIFE. And, may someone come forward to help us insert discipled and discipling to be accepted in spell check options automatically as demonized and demonizing are so easily accepted, already!

Faith Walk and Discipleship

May we find time for our expressions to be similar, when we speak to one another confirming 'Peace be with you' as we depart for the Peace passes all understanding! God has confirmed when I have nothing else to say, tell the person "Bless you" for then the Holy Spirit will remain with them and do a work beyond what I could 'in that moment' for them.

Become Ready to Take On Assignments

As Jesus taught us to pray for God's (not man's) kingdom to come and God's will to be done so it shall become on earth as it is in heaven, I trust you realize it was always God's desire for us to 'get a life license' so we know how to proceed in our life and we know how to live an 'extra' ordinary life.

The process of comprehending God's Storehouse Principle is exactly the same.

With God's guidance by the Holy Spirit, we will always be able to:

1. Expand / store / tithe and understand God's truth, His secret about time,

2. Expand cash flow and enjoy the pay off options vs. budgeting bills,

3. Expand the plan to have time to plan a tithe of all,

4. Expand our skills, talents, and abilities, to bless more people,

5. Expand the foundation / base of our life: people, network, resources,

6. Expand our daily LIFE plan with 'Balanced Life Game', *

7. Expand our LIFE with continued discipleship and new assignments,

* God provides the structure to view all of life within a simple game board format.

The plan for each day can be completed within moments each morning.

Bottom line: It becomes second nature for us to plan and implement a tithe from all that we are and have while we are living a LIFE aligned with and blessed by *God's Storehouse Principle.*

A personal note 'just between us'

We learned an African worship song, a very special and simple message. It was shared by the praise and worship team from Bishop Duncan William's church:

ONE MORE TIME

ONE MORE TIME

HE HAS ALLOWED US TO COME TOGETHER

ONE MORE TIME

By the time we sang it for the third time, there was not a dry eye in the house!

I look forward to hearing from you, and hearing your details about the 'Faith Walk' you are experiencing, or you have experienced! Until we meet, speak and / or email the next ONE MORE TIME, enjoy the journey(s) shared in this book and the journey(s) God is and will continue to take you on! Write to me and share the testimonies of the glorious work our Lord is doing in your life. Until the next ONE MORE TIME our Lord brings us together, as always, HIS Best!

Sheila

Email: HISBest4us@aol.com

*Use the Subject Line: **God's Storehouse Principle***

Ephesians 2:19-22 *We are no longer foreigners and aliens, but fellow citizens... members of God's household, built on the foundation of the apostles and prophets, with Christ Jesus himself as the chief cornerstone. In Him the whole building is joined together and rises to become a holy temple in the Lord. And in Him you too are being built together to become a dwelling in which God lives by His Spirit.*
II Corinthians 12:14-15. (a) *"Now, I am ready to visit you...what I want is not your possessions but you...So I will very gladly spend for you everything I have and expend myself as well."*
II Corinthians 13:11-14. *Aim for perfection ... be of one mind, live in peace, and the God of love and peace will be with you. May the grace of the Lord Jesus Christ, and the love of God, and the fellowship of the Holy Spirit be with you all.*

About the Author, Sheila Holm

God's Storehouse Principle is based upon God's orchestration of all arrangements while God took Sheila's hand and traveled with her while equipping and training her and confirming It's A Faith Walk! The book by the title is a brief summary of about seven months of Sheila's three year journey after she surrendered and walked hand in hand with God, guided by the Holy Spirit each step of the way.

God has taken Sheila around the globe, going church to church, business to business, nation to nation. He directs her path to speak life into each situation whether God sends people to her to be re-encouraged or he asks her to pray with a pastor, the church, or someone in a store or a restaurant, etc. He fulfills upon his promises within the scriptures. He has equipped and trained her. God:

- Sends her forth without an extra coin or tunic.
- Arranges flights and accommodations in each nation.
- Introduces her before she arrives.
- Lifts her up and encourages her.
- Seats her before governors and kings.
- Fills her as an empty vessel.
- Shares His wisdom and word of knowledge.
- Blesses and heals the people in her path.
- Comforts her and re-encourages her.
- Touches people individually in conferences/multitude.
- Speaks through her with power and authority.
- Addresses situations the body of Christ is facing.
- Speaks through her so the people hear His words in their own language.

Many confirm she walks in the five-fold ministry. She does not use a title because God does the work while He sends her as an apostle and prophet. God orchestrates all arrangements for her to preach, teach, and evangelize.

Invitations to preach resulted in this book: **God's Storehouse Principle** with Foreword by Bishop George Dallas McKinney. The secular version of the book is **Balanced Life Game** with Foreword by Ken Blanchard.

When she preaches, God confirms that if churches will begin to shift from world based plans to God's plan by operating within **God's Storehouse Principle**, the church will be able to declare the church is blessed and then God's blessings will begin flow to / through people, families & communities.

God has confirmed the scriptures again and again which confirm we are to be as wise as serpents yet gentle as doves. Sheila often admits the enemy has provided many opportunities for God's deeper training and her expanded growth.

She was considered wealthy in the world before the rug was pulled out, but, she says she would not accept a dime for her prior life because God reached out his hand after she was forced on to a 2nd, 3rd, and 4th Social Security and Driver's license number while a case was being developed for federal prosecution of Superior Court Judges and trial attorneys.

Because she brought the truth forward about multiple injustices within the justice system, specifically the judges and attorneys committing fraud 'behind the scenes,' she was promised IF she changed her ID numbers her new record would be protected and she could proceed upon her one, clear and separate record. After two of the three judges and an attorney were sentenced to prison terms for Federal RICO charges, the agents did not concern themselves with the mess they created in Sheila's life: Their demands that she change her ID multiple times caused her to be unable to function in America. Agents ignored the facts.

The agents offered 5th numbers, but, she said, "Enough." She did not know the truth while they were insisting they were protecting her.

A clear and separate record was promised each time, but, the records were all merged together as one record the entire time Therefore, all expenses and effort to continue to receive their protection by not letting anything merge with her prior record was a lie. The costs to re-establish her life and keep her record clear were 'on her dime.' Without a work or credit history, the costs were high and damages in every part of her life were severe. After so many changes she was out of financial and professional options to start her life over one more time. Their only question: "***We just want to know how did you come through all of this and not commit suicide?***" Her answer was simple: "***God.***"

Clearly, she was done following all of their instructions and getting nowhere. Each time the fraud was supposed to be watched on her prior record and kept separate from her current record, it was not kept separate. Plus, code words they required and assigned with each ID change appear as aliases, so she appeared to be the fraudulent one.

Her merged record was accessible to anyone doing a credit or background check. It rendered her helpless for obtaining credit or employment from the world. All of the fraud committed by the Identity thieves is accessible so anyone checking on her background details would not see the record she stated and trusted was her one, clear record. Instead, people and businesses saw pages and pages of fraud so when she was told 'inconsistent record' each time she was not paid for her work, she had no idea what was going on.

God provided the wisdom and after five years of researching and providing the facts to the agents, the fraud division Deputy DA was arrested, convicted and sentenced on felony fraud.

She had already researched the fraud crimes and provided the facts to the agents. She did not know the truth: the agents lied. When she presented the list of errors to the agents, instead of taking one step to help her or clear her record the agents erased her from the system.

Sheila thanks God that her Lord and Savior stepped in and provided His wisdom and word of knowledge to help her figure out and know the truth: how the citizens, plus the credit, financial, and government systems are vulnerable due to policies allowing ID theft fraud to link to legal citizens while ID theft crimes continue without pursuing or prosecuting the criminals unless the name is already on a terrorist list. God reminded Sheila our identity as believers is in Christ: Ephesians 1:4-5, 2:10, along with a long list of scriptures.

God provided the facts and the connections for Sheila to write the Talking Points Memo for the Senate Banking & Finance Committee which they used to develop a new credit bureau and second ID Theft law signed on July 15, 2004. In the midst of the many debacles and repeated, complete devastation, God made a way. God helped Sheila to re-direct all past knowledge into a new career.

Through global travel arranged by God, Sheila became recognized as an International Leadership, Balanced Life Coach. She is known to impact the life of each participant in corporations and conferences around the world. Her unique tools and techniques evoke immediate, positive, bottom-line strategies because they include the wisdom of God.

Her ID theft story regarding the two decades of devastation is briefly described within a film script and a non-fiction book, ***Vulnerable: The Identity Factor.***

During the same two decades, God provided wisdom for her coaching tools and techniques which impact thousands of conference and seminar participants, business leaders, owners and their management teams on each continent.

Due to her dynamic leadership style, staff members and customers immediately recognize the changes in their life, their business, and the positive impact upon their family, peers, industry, and community. Relationships are blessed.

Due to God's word of knowledge being provided, participants consistently acknowledge her ability to ignite dialogue and inquiry throughout their life or business. They are inspired and re-encouraged so leadership immediately emerges within each life and partnership, i.e., with each staff member, their family members, each customer, vendor, and expanding into powerful business relationships, partnerships, and specifically in establishing multiple, profitable strategic alliances (shifting our focus from all transactions being based upon the exchange of a world based currency / money to becoming successful as a community or industry by sharing resources, aka establishing strategic alliances) which have positively catapulted their life, family & business to the next level of success. Then, they are able to bless more people.

Her coaching techniques are based upon **God's Storehouse Principle.** Sheila developed the practical tools while God took her hand and brought her out of the depth of the debacles. She uses the process to help her clients within the same 'balanced life game board' format, causing clients to realize they are actually 'playing the game' in their own life. The simple format confirms that with bit of practice we can shift from world based processes to **God's Storehouse Principle** and live a full, 7/24 life.

Sheila delivers motivational speeches for corporations and conferences around the world. While traveling as a keynote speaker and seminar leader. A brief list of Sheila's speaking and coaching clients include:

- American Society of Training and Development
- EDS
- Chevron
- Executive Forum
- Rotary and Kiwanis International
- National Insurance Brokers and Agents (NIBA)
- Society for Human Resources Management

Sheila has been featured and quoted on MSNBC, KCBS, CNN Industry Watch, and in Inc Magazine and The Business Cube.

She credits God for providing the wisdom and word of knowledge. The plans are God's plans and the success is based upon God's orchestration of the details.

God arranged a journey, confirming **It's A Faith Walk!** and Sheila recently released the book which includes about seven months of their three year adventure. Her faith walk is truly the result of letting God orchestrate her life, a journey which is God's plan for each of us and God's orchestration for Sheila confirms His plan is beyond our human comprehension.

She prays you will embark on a journey with God and be blessed when you live life per ***God's Storehouse Principle***.

Her unique training program caused the American Federal Government to extend an annual contract to her, to provide God's wisdom within a business development course for the Defense industry.

The 100% success rate of the course provided automatic annual contract renewals for both the Defense and Aerospace industries, where industry participants, i.e., General Dynamics, Hughes and Lockheed, benefited.

Sheila has become a published author Her copyrighted course material became the basis of her business book:

Seven Step Business Plan
Foreword by Ken Blanchard
Distributed by Pelican Publishing

It has garnered international recognition. The book became a key part of the Buckminster Fuller Business School for Entrepreneurs program in Kuala Lumpur, Malaysia and Shenzhen, China. In addition, the European Union Chamber of Commerce requires her book within their core curriculum. The book has been translated into the Spanish Language and published in a Latin America edition.

Her ***Balanced Life Game*** includes her popular Keynote Conference topic: ***Networking Through Six Degrees of Separation. Balanced Life Game*** and ***Vulnerable: The Identity Factor*** books are currently in negotiation with Pelican, the same publisher as ***Seven Step Business Plan***.

Sheila is a lifetime member of the San Diego Society for Human Resources Management (SHRM) and she has served on the boards of a long list of professional and community associations. She founded the industry panel and instructed three of the six core courses for the Management Certificate Program at the University of California, San Diego. She founded and operated a California Corporation after she further developed and directed both marketing and human resources departments for major corporations such as: PAC West, National Pen, AVCO and TraveLodge Int'l. She became a SHRM and Greater San Diego Industry Education Council board member while working in both Production & Industrial Relations at SONY Corporation. She chaired a Robotics in Warehousing project which resulted in spending time in each of the SONY plants in Japan.

She was an Education major at Augustana College, became certified in Telecommunications at Palomar College, obtained a BA degree in Management from Pepperdine University and she is an MBA candidate, Southern Illinois Univ. Sheila is actively engaged in numerous community and charitable activities. She has also enjoyed participating in her special interest, high-speed car rallies especially when they are conducted on California mountain routes.

Sheila looks forward to hearing the details of your testimony for the truth about our daily life is *It's A Faith Walk!* and it is a glorious journey when we understand how to bring it all together when we fellowship in one accord and know that we know we are operating according to ***God's Storehouse Principle.***

Write an email to Sheila: HISBest4us@aol.com.
Use the subject line: ***God's Storehouse Principle.***

Made in the USA
Columbia, SC
03 July 2023

19966074R00117